# *Entertaining*

Now everything you serve at the party can be as fun and festive as a Wilton cake! In *Entertaining*, we'll show you how to create appetizers, entrees and desserts with Wilton style — an elegant shell salad for the bridal shower, a complete Wild West chili birthday supper, a strawberry heart tower for your Valentine and much more. Over 75 exciting recipes and ideas perfect for the occasion.

# *Contents*

# Special Occasions

## Bridal Showers

*An inviting brunch buffet features a creamy shrimp and pasta salad molded in a shell shape and individual fruit and cream shell spongecakes.*

## Weddings

*Hearts come together in unforgettable ways: tomato chicken served with an impressive rice mold, three delightful heart appetizers and a stacked heart cake that is the height of romance.*

## Baby Showers

*Bears everywhere! A giant bear sandwich layered with chicken and crabmeat salads, strawbear-ry mini-mousses and cookie place cards... all that's missing is the bearskin rug!*

## Graduation Day

*Three smart ways to entertain with class: Fresh vegetable and pizza breads, tangy potato salad and decorated cakes which salute your favorite student and earn you extra credit.*

## Mother's Day

*Start her day with breakfast in bed—a luxurious zucchini quiche served with date walnut bread warm from the oven. Later, give Mom her present over a sinfully healthy angel food cake swirled with cinnamon and chocolate.*

## Father's Day

*Here's the ideal easy-chair snack that's easy to make ahead: a 3-layer picante dip with chips. And after his favorite dinner, our checkerboard cake will make Dad feel like a king.*

## Picnics

*The basket is brimming: hearty paté sandwiches made from long, crusty loaves of homebaked bread; cool tomato aspic rich with summertime vegetables; and our coconut pineapple cake—a tropical paradise fluffed with cream cheese frosting.*

## Sports Parties

*Fast snacks for all seasons. Kick off halftime with a hero sandwich in football shape. Our tip for watching hoops—pasta salad with rounds of meat and cheese. The baseball sundae has a great lineup of fruit, nuts and toppings.*

# Lemon Dill Shrimp Mold

*Wilton Shell Pan*
*1 lb. peeled and deveined cooked shrimp*
*2 cups dry orzo pasta, cooked and drained*
*1½ cups carrots, sliced and cooked*
*1 package (10 oz.) frozen peas, cooked and drained*
*1 cup coarsely chopped celery*
*½ cup finely chopped fresh parsley*
*2 teaspoons salt*
*3 packets unflavored gelatin*
*¾ cup cold water*
*3 cups light cream*
*1 package (8 ounces) cream cheese, softened*
*¼ teaspoon pepper*
*2 tablespoons lemon juice*
*1 tablespoon dried dill*
*2 teaspoons horseradish*
*1-2 dashes hot pepper sauce*

Spray Shell Pan lightly with vegetable coating spray. Arrange shrimp evenly in pan. Combine orzo, carrots, peas, celery, parsley and salt in large bowl. Soften gelatin in water, heat until clear, cool slightly. Stir cooled gelatin into cream. Combine with cream cheese and remaining ½ teaspoon salt, pepper, lemon juice, dill, horseradish and hot pepper sauce. Pour over orzo mixture. Spoon orzo mixture over shrimp. Cover and refrigerate until firm (several hours or overnight). When mold is firm, run small spatula around edge of mold and invert onto serving tray. Garnish with shrimp, lemon wedge, carrot curls, and dill.

Makes 12-15 servings.

# Heart Scones

*Wilton Nesting Heart Cookie Cutters*
*Wilton Cookie Sheet*
*2 cups flour*
*6 oz. cheddar, grated*
*2 tablespoons sugar*
*3 teaspoons baking powder*
*¼ teaspoon baking soda*
*1 teaspoon salt*
*1 egg, slightly beaten*
*½ cup sour cream*
*¼ cup vegetable oil*
*3 tablespoons milk*

Preheat oven to 425°F. In a medium bowl, combine flour, cheese, sugar, baking powder, baking soda and salt. In separate bowl, mix remaining ingredients. Make a well in flour mixture, add egg mixture and stir until dough clings together. Turn out onto floured surface, knead 10-12 times until smooth. Roll out ⅓ in. thick, cut with heart cutters. Place on ungreased cookie sheet. Bake 15-20 minutes or until brown. Reroll remaining dough and cut additional scones.

Makes 12-15 large scones.

*Shells are the shape of elegance for showers and luncheons. The Wilton Shell Pan will hold its shape through years of special occasions — its quality anodized aluminum construction makes it the perfect pan for beautifully defined gelatin molds, cakes and breads.*

# SHELL SPONGECAKES

*Wilton Mini Shell Pan*
*Wilton Disposable Decorating Bags*
*Wilton Tip 21*
*3 large eggs, room temperature*
*½ cup sugar*
*½ teaspoon Wilton Clear Vanilla*
*½ cup flour, sifted*
*Whipped cream*
*Strawberries, blueberries and blackberries*

Preheat oven to 350°F. Spray pan cavities with vegetable oil spray. Beat eggs and sugar at high speed for approximately 5 minutes, until mixture is very thick and light in color. Beat in vanilla; fold in flour. Fill pans about ⅓ inch from top. Bake for approximately 10 minutes. Remove from oven, run small spatula around top of rim and release immediately. If using one pan, refrigerate batter between baking.

To assemble, place one shell on plate, fill disposable bag with whipped cream and pipe tip 21 shells. Add berries and top shell. Garnish with berries. Spongecakes may be baked one day ahead and kept in a single layer in airtight containers.

Makes 12 shells.

*With the Mini Shell Pan, you can serve a shower of great tastes! Set everyone's place with mini gelatins, individual molded salads, shell rolls, filled cookies—even molded chocolate shells. It's the pan that's filled with possibilities!*

*Wedding*

# Cucumber Hearts

*Wilton Nesting Heart Cookie Cutters*
*Wilton Disposable Decorating Bags*
*Wilton Tip #2110*
*1 large cucumber*
*1 teaspoon horseradish*
*¼ cup sour cream*
*Dill for garnish*

Hot house or seedless cucumbers are easiest to cut; purchase the largest diameter available. Peel and slice cucumber ¼-in. thick; cut with various size Nesting Heart Cutters. Mix sour cream and horseradish, pipe on cucumber slices with a large #2110 star tip. Add dill to garnish.

Makes approximately 3 dozen.

# Smoked Salmon Hearts

*Wilton Nesting Heart Cookie Cutters*
*Wilton Disposable Decorating Bags*
*Wilton Tip #2110*
*1 loaf unsliced white bread*
*2 oz. smoked salmon or trout, sliced thin*
*Dill, sour cream for garnish*

Trim crust and slice bread lengthwise. Roll lightly with rolling pin, cut with various size Nesting Heart Cutters. As bread is cut, it should be covered with plastic wrap or a damp towel. Top with thin slices of salmon. Pipe on sour cream with star tip #2110. Garnish with a sprig of dill.

Makes 4 dozen.

# Green Chili Tarts

***Cornmeal Crust:***
*Wilton Petite Heart Pan*
*1 cup flour*
*½ cup yellow cornmeal*
*¼ teaspoon salt*
*2 oz. cold butter (½ stick)*
*2½ oz. cold cream cheese*
*1 tablespoon cold water*

Preheat oven to 400°F.

In bowl of food processor fitted with metal blade, process flour, cornmeal and salt with 3-4 short pulses. With machine running add pieces of butter and cream cheese one at a time. Stop machine; add tablespoon of cold water. Process until dough just holds together. Form into roll, chill 30 minutes. Divide into 48 chunks. Press into Petite Heart Pan. Prick crusts and bake 10 minutes.

***Tart Filling:***
*2 (4 oz.) cans green chilies, chopped*
*½ small jalapeño pepper, peeled, seeded and finely chopped*
*¼ cup milk*
*1 egg*
*¼ teaspoon salt*
*Dash of pepper*
*2 oz. sharp cheddar, shredded*
*2 oz. Monterrey Jack, shredded*

Mix all ingredients except cheeses. In each tart crust place a small amount of each cheese. With a small spoon, add egg chili mixture. Bake for 15-20 additional minutes or until browned. Serve at room temperature with salsa (see recipe on p. 31). Tarts can be made the day before — just cool, cover and refrigerate; reheat briefly in a 350°F oven.

*The Petite Heart Pan is also a natural for Valentine desserts. Try the Mini Chocolate Cherry Tarts recipe on the label!*

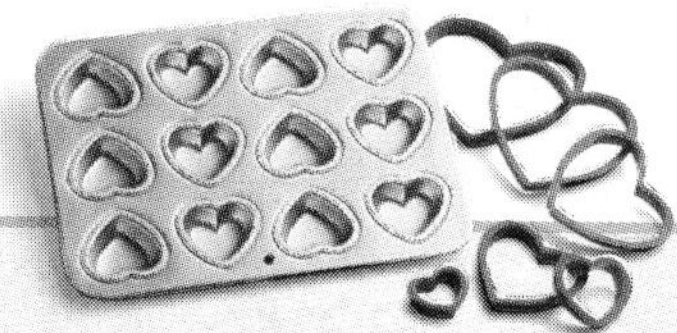

# Tomato Chicken Over Rice

*Wilton Embossed Heart Pan*
*4 tablespoons olive oil, divided*
*3½ lbs. boneless chicken pieces, cut in strips*
*1 lb. mushrooms, thinly sliced*
*1 cup onion, chopped*
*1 cup green pepper, chopped*
*4 cloves garlic, crushed*
*1 (28 oz.) can crushed tomatoes*
*1 (14½ oz.) can chicken broth*
*1 teaspoon salt*
*½ teaspoon black pepper*
*2 teaspoons fresh basil*
*3 tablespoons tomato paste*
*3½ cups rice, cooked (to make 11 cups) do not use instant rice*
*Plum tomatoes, whole mushrooms, basil leaves for garnish*

Saute chicken strips in one tablespoon oil very quickly until tender, but still moist. Remove and set aside. Sauté sliced mushrooms, approximately 10 minutes. Reserve. Sauté chopped onion and green pepper in 3 tablespoons olive oil until limp and transparent, but not browned. Add crushed garlic and sauté briefly. Stir in tomatoes, chicken broth, seasonings and tomato paste. Simmer about 20 minutes on low heat. Combine chicken and mushrooms with tomato mixture.

Cook rice. Lightly oil Embossed Heart Pan; pack hot rice into pan. Turn out immediately onto serving tray. Garnish with sauteéd whole mushrooms, flowers made from plum tomatoes, and basil leaves.

Makes 18-20 servings.

***To Make A Tomato Rose:***
Place a firm ripe plum tomato stem-side down on cutting board. Cut a thin base from the tomato with a sharp paring knife, leaving it attached. Hold the tomato, stem-side down. Cut, in a zigzag motion, a thin continuous ⅓-½ in. wide spiral of skin, starting from cut base to the top of tomato. Lay this spiral, skin side down. Starting at the bottom end, roll up strip completely. To finish the rose, spread "petals" gently apart for a realistic look, using a toothpick.

*The Embossed Heart Pan turns a 2-layer cake mix into a masterpiece. The raised heart center is the perfect platform for your cake's fresh fruit and whipped cream accompaniment. Baking and decorating instructions are included on the label.*

## Heart Romance Cake

*Wilton 9 in. and 12 in. Heart Pans*
*Wilton Disposable Decorating Bags*
*Wilton Tips 1, 3, 18, 19, 101s, 352*
*Wilton Pink, Moss Green Icing Colors*
*Wilton Flower Nail No. 9*
*Wilton Dowel Rods*
*Wilton Meringue Powder*
*Wilton Crystal-Look Base*
*Wilton Love's Duet Ornament (Black Tux)*
*Royal Icing (see recipe on Meringue Powder label)*
*Buttercream Icing (see pg. 19)*

NOTE: For instructions on specific decorating techniques, see the current Wilton Yearbook of Cake Decorating.

Using royal icing, make 36 tip 101s roses with tip 3 bases. Make extras to allow for breakage, and let dry.

Position 2-layer cakes on individual foil-covered boards cut to fit. Ice smooth in buttercream icing. Dowel rod bottom heart, stack cakes, position on serving platter.

Beginning at point of heart cakes, dot mark every 2 in. along top edge of both hearts, and also along bottom edge of 12 in. heart. Using tip 3, pipe triple drop strings between marks on both tiers, and scallops on top of 12 in. tier. Cover top of 9 in. heart and drop string areas with tip 1 cornelli lace. On 12 in tier, pipe tip 19 zigzag puff bottom border between marks, add tip 3 dots and fleur-de-lis; on 9 in. tier, pipe tip 18 bottom shell border. Position Crystal-Look Base on cake top. Add roses and tip 352 leaves along edge of Crystal-Look Base and at bottom border of 12 in tier. At reception, position ornament on cake top.

Makes 72 servings (9 in. and 12 in. heart together as shown). 12 in. heart alone serves 48.

## Sweetheart Cookie Favors

*Wilton 6-Pc. Nesting Heart Cookie Cutters (3¾-in. size used)*
*Wilton Tips 3, 101s, 352*
*Wilton Flower Nail No. 9*
*Wilton Pink and Moss Green Icing Colors*
*Wilton Bomboniere!® Pink 5/16 in. Instant Bow Ribbon*
*1 cup butter*
*1 cup sugar*
*1 large egg*
*1 tsp. vanilla*
*2 tsps. baking powder*
*3 cups flour*
*Drinking straw*
*Royal Icing (see recipe on Meringue Powder label)*
*Buttercream Icing (see pg. 19)*

Preheat oven to 400°F. In a large bowl, cream butter and sugar with an electric mixer. Beat in egg and vanilla. Add baking powder and flour, one cup at a time, mixing after each addition. The dough will be very stiff; blend last flour in by hand. Do not chill dough.

Divide dough into 2 balls. On a floured surface, roll each ball into a circle approximately 12 inches in diameter and ⅛ in. thick. Cut out cookies. Use a drinking straw dipped in flour to cut opening for bow.

Bake cookies on an ungreased cookie sheet on middle rack of oven for 6-7 minutes, or until cookies are lightly browned. Cool completely before decorating. If opening has baked together, run toothpick or skewer through while cookie is warm.

With royal icing, make tip 101s roses with tip 3 base. Let dry. With buttercream icing, pipe tip 3 names on cookie. Cut 13 in. lengths of ribbon and tie bow through opening in cookie. Position rose with dot of icing and add tip 352 buttercream leaves.

Makes 24 cookies.

*Look at all you can create with versatile Wilton Heart Pans! Use the techniques explained in our Annual Yearbook of Cake Decorating to create the lovely effects shown above — roses, cornelli lace, fancy stringwork and more. You'll also find great ways to decorate on every pan label.*

Laura
&
Paul

*Baby Shower*

# Layered Bear Sandwich

*Wilton Huggable Bear Pan*
*4½ cups all-purpose flour, divided*
*2 teaspoons salt*
*2 packages quick rise yeast*
*1½ cups milk*
*1½ cups water*
*¼ cup honey*
*¼ cup vegetable oil*
*4 cups whole wheat flour*

Combine 2¼ cups all-purpose flour, salt and yeast in large mixing bowl. Heat milk, water, honey and oil until hot to touch (125°F-130°F). Gradually add to dry ingredients; beat 2 minutes at medium speed of mixer, scraping bowl occasionally. Add 1 cup all-purpose flour; beat at high speed 2 minutes, scraping bowl occasionally. With spoon, stir in whole wheat flour and enough additional all-purpose flour to make stiff dough. Knead on lightly floured surface until smooth and elastic, about 6 to 8 minutes. Place in greased bowl, turning to grease top. Cover; let rest 10 minutes. Roll dough out into approximate shape of bear. Press into greased Huggable Bear Pan. Cover; let rise in warm place until doubled in size, about 30 minutes. Bake at 375°F for 35 minutes or until done. Remove from pan; cool on wire rack. Trim crown if necessary, split into 3 layers, spread one layer with chicken salad; one with crabmeat, reassemble. Decorate with piped softened cream cheese, using tip #21. Make tie with shaved carrots, green onion strips (softened in microwave for 30 seconds) and dill.

Makes 16-20 servings.

***Chicken Salad***

*3 large boneless skinless chicken breasts (approximately 9 ounces)*
*½ cup finely chopped celery*
*2 finely chopped green onions, including 2 in. of green top*
*1 cup chopped water chestnuts*
*2 tablespoons diced pimentos*
*1 tablespoon finely chopped parsley*
*¾ cup mayonnaise*
*¼ cup sour cream*
*½ teaspoon each, salt, white pepper*

Simmer chicken breasts in ½ cup water until tender or cook in microwave approximately 9 minutes or until done. Remove; cool and chop. Combine in mixing bowl with celery, onion, water chestnuts, pimento and parsley. In separate bowl, blend mayonnaise, sour cream and seasonings. Stir into chicken mixture.

***Crabmeat Salad***

*12 oz. imitation crab meat blend, chopped*
*½ cup finely chopped celery*
*2 finely chopped green onions, including 2 in. of green top*
*½ cup chopped green pepper*
*½ cup crushed pineapple, drained*
*4 oz. cream cheese, softened*
*¼ cup sour cream*
*¼ cup mayonnaise*
*½ teaspoon white pepper*

Combine crabmeat, celery, onion, green pepper and pineapple in mixing bowl. In a separate bowl, blend cream cheese, sour cream, mayonnaise and pepper until smooth. Blend dressing mixture into crabmeat mixture.

*Huggable Bear is just one way to create a complete "baby bear" shower. Try individual breads in our Mini Bear Pan or cookies and candy made from delightful Wilton cutters and molds!*

*Baby Shower*

# Strawberry Mousse

*Wilton 6-Cavity Mini Bear Pan*
*Wilton Disposable Decorating Bags*
*Wilton Tip 2*
*1 (6 oz.) 8 serving size package strawberry gelatin*
*1 (10 oz.) package frozen sliced strawberries with sugar*
*2 cups boiling water*
*1 cup heavy whipping cream, divided*

Dissolve gelatin in boiling water. Place frozen strawberries in food processor, chop. Strain out seeds. Stir strained strawberries into dissolved gelatin. Allow to thicken slightly, about 1½ hours. Whip cream; reserve ⅓ cup to pipe faces. Fold remaining cream into strawberry mixture. Carefully stir until smooth and mixed well. Pour into 6-Cavity Mini Bear Pan. Chill until set. Unmold by running small spatula around edge of pan cavities. Fill Decorating Bag with remaining whipped cream and pipe eyes, nose and bow with tip 2.

Makes 6 bears.

# Cub Cookies

*Wilton Nesting Bear Cookie Cutters (largest cutter used)*
*Wilton Disposable Decorating Bags*
*Wilton Tip 2*
*Wilton Pink, Sky Blue Icing Colors*
*½ cup butter*
*1 cup sugar*
*1 egg*
*1 teaspoon baking powder*
*1¾ cups flour*
*1 tablespoon milk*
*½ teaspoon vanilla*
*¼ teaspoon salt*
*Buttercream icing*

Preheat oven to 375°F. Cream butter and sugar, add egg and mix. Add remaining ingredients and mix until smooth. Refrigerate 2 hours. Roll out ⅛ in. thick on lightly floured surface, dip cutter in flour before each use. Place on ungreased cookie sheet. These cookies puff up and spread slightly; be sure to leave at least 2 inches between cookies. Bake 12-15 minutes or until browned. Remove from sheet and cool.

Using tip 2 and buttercream icing, pipe dot eyes and nose and string tie on each cookie.

***Buttercream Icing***
*½ cup solid vegetable shortening*
*½ cup butter or margarine*
*1 teaspoon Wilton Clear Vanilla*
*4 cups sifted confectioners sugar (approx. 1 lb)*
*2 tablespoons milk**

Cream butter and shortening with electric mixer. Add vanilla. Gradually add sugar, one cup at a time, beating well on medium speed. Scrape sides and bottom of bowl often. When all sugar has been mixed in, icing will appear dry. Add milk and beat at medium speed until light and fluffy. Keep icing covered with a damp cloth until ready to use. For best results, keep icing bowl in refrigerator when not in use. Refrigerated in an airtight container, this icing can be stored 2 weeks. Re-whip before using.

Makes 3 cups

*Add 3-4 tablespoons milk per recipe to thin for icing cake or cookies.

*Instead of one big cake, try our Mini Bear Pan for individual treats everyone can enjoy. One mix makes 16-20 bears perfect for kids' birthdays — they're easy and fun to decorate too! And don't forget Wilton Nesting Bear Cookie Cutters bring smiles to everyday snacking.*

# Lucky Potato Salad

*Wilton Horseshoe Pan*
*4½ lbs. red potatoes, cooked in jackets, peeled, cubed (3 medium potatoes equal 1 lb.)*
*¼ cup red onion, finely chopped*
*¼ cup green onion, finely chopped*
*2¼ cups celery, coarsely chopped*
*½ cup green pepper, chopped*
*1 tablespoon salt or to taste*
*1 teaspoon black pepper*
*2 tablespoons minced fresh parsley*
*½ teaspoon dry mustard*
*2½ cups mayonnaise*
*1½ cups sour cream*
*4 hard boiled eggs, chopped*

Combine potatoes, onions, celery and green pepper. Sprinkle minced parsley, salt and black pepper over all. Combine dry mustard with mayonnaise and sour cream, mix well. Pour over potato mixture. Add chopped eggs and gently mix. Line Horseshoe Pan with plastic wrap. Spoon potato salad and firmly pack into pan. Unmold onto large serving platter. Serve with rolled meats, cheeses and condiments, like the sauces below. Garnish meats with pimento bows.

Makes 15-18 servings.

# Meat Sauces

***Horseradish Sauce***
*½ cup whipping cream*
*3 tablespoons prepared horseradish sauce*

Whip cream until soft mounds form. Fold in prepared horseradish sauce. Refrigerate until ready to serve. This will keep one day covered tightly in the refrigerator. Stir before serving. Do not use sweetened whipping cream or frozen topping.

Makes 1 cup.

***Mustard Sauce***
*1 cup plain yogurt*
*3 tablespoons prepared Dijon mustard*

Mix yogurt and mustard. Cover and refrigerate.

Makes 1 cup.

*The Horseshoe Pan is perfect for good luck occasions all year long. Great for birthdays, bon voyage, even Christmas stockings! See the label for great decorating ideas.*

# Unique Pizzas

***CRUST***

*Performance Pans™*
*9x13 in. Sheet Pan or*
*10½ x 15 in. Jelly Roll/ Cookie Pan*
*1 package active dry yeast*
*¾ cup warm water*
*1 tablespoon sugar*
*1 tablespoon olive oil*
*½ teaspoon salt*
*2-2¼ cups flour*

In mixing bowl, stir yeast into warm water until dissolved. Add sugar, oil and salt. Stir in 1½ cups of flour. Gradually add remaining flour to form a soft dough. Turn onto a lightly floured surface; knead until smooth and elastic, about 4-5 minutes. Shape dough into a ball and place in oiled bowl; turn dough to coat. Cover and let rise in warm place for 1½ hours or until doubled in bulk. Punch dough down; knead 2 minutes on a floured surface. Roll or stretch dough into rectangle to match size of pan. Place in oiled pan. Follow recipes below for rising and baking directions.

***FOCCACIA***

*1 recipe crust*
*1 large eggplant, sliced ⅛-in. thick*
*1 medium onion, thinly sliced*
*¼ cup plus 2 tablespoons olive oil*
*3 cloves garlic, crushed*
*6 plum tomatoes*
*¼ teaspoon black pepper*
*½ teaspoon oregano*

Preheat oven to 450°F. Place eggplant in strainer or colander, sprinkle with 1 tablespoon salt, let set 20 minutes. Blot on paper towel. Sauté eggplant and onion together with ¼ cup olive oil, add garlic, continue sautéing until onion is limp and transparent, but not brown. In the meantime, brush 9 x 13 in. Sheet Pan with 1 tablespoon olive oil, roll out bread dough and fit into pan. Let rise for 30 minutes, bake 10 minutes. Brush 1 tablespoon olive oil on crust. Place tomato slices on slightly baked crust, add sautéed vegetables, sprinkle black pepper and oregano on top. Bake an additional 15-20 minutes.

Makes 12 servings.

***FRESH VEGETABLE PIZZA***

*1 recipe crust*
*2 cups grated mozzarella cheese*
*¼ lb. (about 6) ripe Italian plum tomatoes, sliced ⅛" thick*
*3 tablespoons olive oil*
*½ lb. mushrooms, sliced*
*1 small onion, sliced*
*½ red pepper, cut in strips*
*½ green pepper, cut in strips*
*1 teaspoon fresh basil*
*Salt & pepper to taste*

Preheat oven to 450°F. Lightly oil bottom of 10½ x 15 in. Jelly Roll/Cookie Pan. Roll out dough to fit pan (this is a thin crust). Place dough in pan. Let rise 20 minutes. Sauté mushrooms, onions, red & green peppers in 2 tablespoons olive oil. Place mozzarella on crust, add tomatoes and sautéed vegetables. Sprinkle with basil, salt and pepper. Dribble on remaining olive oil. Bake for 20 minutes or until crust is brown and cheese is melted.

Makes 12 servings.

*Pizza's not only for round pans. Large jelly roll or sheet pans make it easy to serve pizza to a crowd. Use these quality Wilton aluminum pans to achieve the even heating and browning that results in a perfect, crunchy crust every time.*

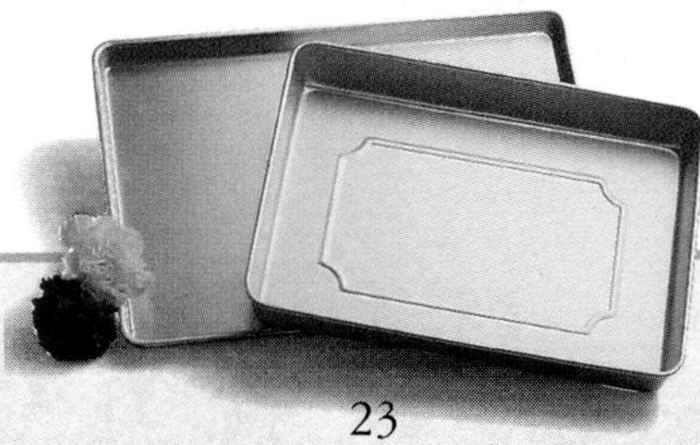

*Graduation Day*

# TOP OF THE CLASS

*Performance Pans™ 12 in. Square Pan*
*Wilton 8 in. Ring Mold Pan*
*Wilton Numbers Pan Set*
*Wilton Disposable Decorating Bags*
*Wilton Candy Melts™* (1 bag Red needed)*
*Tips 3, 14, 16, 32*
*Wilton Red (No-Taste) Icing Color*
*Wilton Cake Boards, Fanci-Foil Wrap*
*Wilton Happy Graduate Topper*
*Dowel Rods*
*Buttercream Icing (see pg. 19)*
*Fresh flowers and greenery*
**brand confectionery coating*

NOTE: For specific cake decorating techniques, see the current Wilton Yearbook of Cake Decorating.

To mold candy plaque numbers: Melt Candy Melts™ following package directions. Pour melted candy into center of pan. For control, use a disposable decorating bag fitted with tip 2 or snip off a very small opening at end of disposable bag. Tap pan gently on counter to break up bubbles and spread candy evenly over bottom (approximately 1/4 in. thick). Place pan in refrigerator for approximately 5 to 10 minutes. Unmold onto hand or soft towel (tap pan gently, if necessary). Set aside.

Position 2-layer square and ring cakes on individual foil-covered boards; ice smooth with buttercream icing. Position 3 dowel rods in square tier and stack cakes. Divide bottom of square and round tiers at 2 in. intervals and mark height for upright shells as follows. On square tier mark each side from center—one 1 in., two 1 1/2 in., then two 2 in., then corners full length. Mark round as for square, leaving 4 in. open at front and reversing order for back of cake. Using tip 32, pipe upright shells at marks; add tip 32 stars for bottom border. Add tip 3 double drop strings and dot trim. Edge top borders with tip 16 shells. Add tip 3 message. Edge candy numbers with tip 14 shells and position numbers on cake. Position Happy Graduate and fresh flowers.

Makes 54 servings.

# CHOCOLATE WALNUT HONOR ROLL

***Cake Roll:***
*Wilton 10½ x 15½ in. Jelly Roll/Cookie Pan*
*3 large eggs, separated*
*2 teaspoons water*
*½ cup sugar*
*1 cup flour*
*1 teaspoon baking powder*
*¾ cup ground walnuts*
*Sugar to sprinkle*

***Filling:***
*1 cup heavy cream*
*2 tblsps. confectioners sugar*
*½ cup shaved chocolate*
*½ cup walnut pieces*
*1 cup whipping cream, whipped*

Preheat oven to 400°F.

**Cake:**
Line jelly roll pan with parchment or wax paper. Grease liberally and dust with flour.

Beat egg whites with water until very stiff. Gradually add sugar, a spoonful at a time, beating until thick and glossy. Whisk egg yolks, add to the whites, then carefully mix in baking powder and flour; fold in ground walnuts. Turn mixture into prepared pan and level top. Bake for 12-14 minutes.

When baked, turn out onto a sheet of wax paper sprinkled with a little sugar. Roll from the short end like a jelly roll, keeping the paper inside. Cool.

**Filling:**
Whip cream and sugar until thick; fold in walnut pieces and chocolate. Unroll cake and carefully remove paper. Spread with cream mixture and re-roll. Ice with whipped cream.

Makes 12-14 servings.

**Candy Clay Bow:**
Before serving, decorate cake with pre-made Candy Clay Bow. See ingredients and instructions, pg. 56.

*For elaborate entertaining or simple, everyday baking—you need a library of essential Wilton pans.*

Class of
95

## ZUCCHINI QUICHE

***Crust:***
*Wilton 9-in. Springform Pan*
*2 cups flour*
*1/2 teaspoon salt*
*3/4 cups cold butter cut into 1/2-in. pieces*
*3 tablespoons cold water*

***Quiche Filling***
*3/4 cup flour*
*1 teaspoon salt*
*3/4 teaspoon fresh ground pepper*
*1/3 cup grated Swiss cheese*
*1 cup (4 oz.) grated cheddar cheese*
*1 cup (one medium) diced onion*
*2 1/2 cups shredded zucchini*
*5 eggs, beaten lightly*

Preheat oven to 450°F.

Add salt to flour. Cut butter into flour with pastry blender, two knives, or food processor until it resembles coarse meal. Add water a small amount at a time and stir or process until dough holds together in a ball. Form into a smooth ball; roll on lightly floured surface. May be wrapped and refrigerated until ready to roll. Roll into 13 in. diameter and fit into Springform Pan. Press against sides and flute. Prick crust with fork. Cover crust with waxed paper, fill with dry beans or pie weights to keep crust flat. Bake 15 minutes. Remove from oven and fill with quiche filling. Return to oven and immediately turn temperature down to 350°F. Bake 1 hour 10 minutes to 1 hour 30 minutes or until quiche is brown and firm to the touch.

***Quiche Filling***

Mix flour, salt and pepper, stir in cheeses, onion and zucchini, add eggs and stir until well blended. Pour into prepared crust.

Makes 6 servings.

## DATE WALNUT BREAD

*Wilton 7 in. Angel Food Pan*
*3 3/4 cups unbleached all-purpose flour*
*1/2 cup sugar*
*1 tablespoon cinnamon*
*1 package dry yeast*
*3/4 cup milk*
*1/2 cup butter*
*2 large eggs*

***Filling***
*2 tablespoons butter, melted*
*1/2 cup finely chopped dates*
*1/2 cup chopped walnuts*
*2 tablespoons sugar*
*1 tablespoon cinnamon*

You will need a counter top mixer for this bread, it is difficult to mix by hand or with a small hand mixer.

In a large mixer bowl, combine flour, sugar, cinnamon and yeast. Mix well. Combine milk and butter in a small saucepan, heat on medium until very warm (120°F-130°F). Slowly add to dry ingredients while mixing; mix well. Add eggs and beat dough 2 minutes; dough will be soft. Cover and let raise until doubled in bulk. Punch down and knead 4-5 times on well floured surface. Roll into approximately 15 x 9 inch rectangle. Brush with melted butter, sprinkle with remaining filling ingredients. Roll from long width, pinch seams together. Grease or spray with a vegetable oil pan spray 7 in. Angel Food Pan. Coil bread roll around center tube. Cover, let raise until doubled or 1 in. from top of pan. With scissors, snip 4-5 slashes on top. Bake in a preheated 350°F oven for 30-40 minutes until brown and hollow sounding when tapped. Cool 5 minutes, remove from pan. Serve warm or at room temperature. To freeze, let cool completely, wrap airtight.

Makes one 7 in. bread.

*Better designed pans mean better baking results. Wilton Springform Pans feature a waffled removable bottom to prevent sticking of delicate quiches and cheesecakes. Our 7-in. Angel Food Pan is a convenient smaller size, with legs that balance the pan for more efficient cooling of angel food cake.*

MOM

# Cinnamon Chocolate Swirl Angel Food Cake

*Wilton 10-in. Angel Food Pan*
*1½ cups sifted cake flour*
*1¾ cups sugar, divided*
*1 teaspoon ground cinnamon*
*12 large egg whites (about 1 cup) at room temperature*
*¼ teaspoon salt*
*1½ teaspoons cream of tartar*
*1 teaspoon Wilton Clear Vanilla*
*4 tablespoons cocoa powder*
*2 tablespoons granulated sugar*
*Strawberries*
*Coffee ice cream*

Preheat oven to 325°F. Sift flour with ¾ cup of sugar and cinnamon three times; set aside. In a large bowl, beat egg whites and salt with electric mixer until foamy. Add cream of tartar and beat until soft peaks form. Gradually beat in remaining 1 cup sugar, sprinkling ¼ cup at a time, beating well after each addition until soft peaks form when beater is withdrawn. With a large rubber scraper or whisk, gently fold in vanilla extract. Sift ¼ of flour mixture at a time over egg whites; gently fold in with over and under motion after each addition. Fold mixture about 10 additional strokes after last addition until flour mixture is well blended. Gently transfer ⅓ of the batter to ungreased 10-in. Angel Food Pan. Mix cocoa powder and sugar; sprinkle ½ of the mixture over batter. Transfer second third of batter, gently spreading over cocoa mixture. Sprinkle with remaining ½ of cocoa mixture. Top with last third of cake batter, spreading gently. With a spatula or knife, cut through batter gently to make swirl. Bake on lower rack at 325°F for 55-60 minutes or until top is browned and cake tester comes out clean. Invert pan on counter to cool cake thoroughly (about 2 hours). Loosen cake with spatula from pan; remove from pan. Serve with strawberries and coffee ice cream.

*Cholesterol-free angel food cake is being served more often by great entertainers! And Wilton Angel Food Pans, in a variety of sizes, give you so many exciting ways to make this smart dessert. Try it with fresh strawberries, lemon sauce or boiled icing for a healthy way to indulge!*

# Molded Mexicali Dip

*Wilton 10 in. Ring Mold Pan*

***Cheese Layer***

*2 packages unflavored gelatin*
*½ cup lemon juice*
*3 (8 oz.) packages cream cheese, softened*
*1 cup sour cream*
*1 (1.25 oz.) package dry taco seasoning mix*

***Avocado Layer***

*2 envelopes unflavored gelatin*
*1½ cups cold water, divided*
*⅓ cup thick and chunky picante sauce*
*2 tablespoons lemon juice*
*1 teaspoon salt, or to taste*
*2 teaspoons grated onion*
*¾ cup sour cream*
*¾ cup mayonnaise*
*2 cups mashed ripe avocado (about 4 large)*

Spray Wilton 10 in. Ring Mold Pan with vegetable pan spray. Prepare cheese layer: Add unflavored gelatin to lemon juice, let stand 2-5 minutes to soften. Heat just until clear. Set aside. In a medium mixing bowl, beat softened cream cheese until smooth. Add sour cream and taco seasoning. Mix well. Add gelatin mixture and blend. Pour into prepared mold and refrigerate while making avocado layer.

Prepare avocado layer: Add gelatin to ½ cup cold water, let stand 2-5 minutes to soften, heat until clear, set aside. Mix remaining ingredients except avocado until smooth. Add avocado as soon as mashed to prevent discoloring. Mix. Add gelatin mixture, mix. Pour over cream cheese layer in pan. Refrigerate 4 hours until set or overnight. To unmold, run thin bladed knife around outside and inside of ring. Dip in hot water 3-4 seconds and unmold. Serve with salsa in center.

This recipe molds well in any of Wilton's shaped pans. Try a Football or Horseshoe for different occasions.

Makes 25 appetizer size servings.

***Salsa:***

*3 cans (28 oz.) Italian tomatoes, drained and coarsely chopped*
*2 cans (4 oz.) chopped, drained green chilies*
*1 jalapeño pepper, chopped*
*½ bunch cilantro, chopped (approximately 1 cup chopped)*
*1 bunch green onions, chopped*
*1 medium white onion, chopped*
*2 garlic cloves, finely chopped*
*Salt and pepper to taste*

***To Make Salsa***

Combine salsa ingredients and chill overnight. Will keep covered in refrigerator one week.

Makes approximately 5 cups.

*The Ring Mold is ideal for letting party guests serve themselves — the middle makes a convenient place for dips and toppings. Bake a bread ring served with a spinach dip center... or, for an elegant dessert, mold a layered ice cream circle served with a container of chocolate sauce in the middle.*

# Checkerboard Cake

*Wilton 8 in. Square Pans (3 used)*
*Wilton Candy Melts™* White and Lt. Cocoa*
*Wilton Tip 21*
*Wilton Disposable Decorating Bags*
*2 (16 oz.) packages yellow or white cake mix*
*2 oz. unsweetened baking chocolate, melted*
*Buttercream Icing (see pg. 19)*
*Cocoa Powder*
*Waxed paper, cut into sixteen 1 in. squares*

**Brand confectionery coating*

Prepare pans: Using the side of 8 in. square pan as a guide, cut 9 dividers of heavy, clean paperboard each approximately 8 x 2 in. (the back of a tablet of paper works well). Each pan will use 3 dividers for four sections of batter, check to be certain pieces fit snugly in pans. Grease and flour pans, then position dividers equally across pan, tape to fit securely. Note: Dividers and tape will be removed before baking. Set pans aside.

Preheat oven to 350°F, and separately prepare cake mixes according to package directions. Add melted chocolate to one mix. (Or you may use a yellow and a chocolate cake mix, but note that different flavors of cake mix yield different amounts. You will need to use equal amounts of yellow and chocolate batter to achieve the desired checkerboard effect for this cake.) Divide each flavor of batter into 6 portions. If you have 6 cups of batter, each section will take 1 cup of batter. Pour into prepared pans, alternating colors. Because the pans are square and can be turned to stack, you do not need to be concerned which color you start with. If you have only 2 pans, refrigerate remaining batter between baking. Remove dividers and tape, bake according to package directions. Cool 10 minutes in pans, remove, trim crowns and cool at least two additional hours before icing and decorating.

Stack and fill the 3 layers, aligning alternating color stripes. When serving this cake, you will need to cut across the stripe to achieve the checkerboard effect; mark that serving side with a toothpick—do this before icing. Ice cake top and sides smooth, allow icing to crust slightly. Position waxed paper squares on cake top to form checkerboard pattern; leave ½ in. on edge for border. Dust cake top with cocoa, carefully remove waxed paper squares. Position Candy Melts™. Pipe tip 21 bottom and top shell borders with buttercream icing.

Makes 24 servings.

*Wilton Square Pans are great gift-makers! Use them for baking mouth-watering brownies, bar cookies and cakes—more meaningful because they're homemade! Why not decorate a cake to look just like a present? Stack cake tiers, ice smooth and tie on a real bow!*

Dad

# Sandwiches For A Crowd

***Paté Loaf:***
*Wilton Long Loaf Pan*
*3 lbs. ground chuck*
*3 lbs. ground pork*
*5 slices fresh bread, torn in chunks*
*1 cup milk*
*3 eggs*
*1 teaspoon salt*
*1 teaspoon Italian Seasoning*
*½ teaspoon pepper*
*¼ cup pine nuts*
*1 roasted red pepper, sliced*
*1 roasted yellow pepper, sliced*
*Fresh basil leaves*

Preheat oven to 350°F. In a large bowl, mix meats, bread, milk, eggs, salt, seasonings and pepper. To test seasoning, fry a small patty in skillet. If needed, add more seasonings. Mix in pine nuts. In Long Loaf Pan, place layer of meat about 1 in. deep, layer strips of roasted pepper and basil leaves. Repeat layers until all meat is used. Loaf should be a mosaic when cut. Cover Loaf Pan with foil. Place in 12 x 18 x 2 in. pan with hot water to 1 in. depth. This is easier to handle if long loaf is placed in sheet pan on oven rack, then add hot water to 1 in. depth. Bake approximately 2 hours or until meat thermometer registers 170°F. Remove, pour off liquid from loaf, place smaller pan on top, add weight (two 1 lb. cans), refrigerate. This will make a paté loaf. This recipe can also be baked as a regular meat loaf. For meatloaf, do not cover or put in water.

***Bread:***
*Wilton Long Loaf Pan*
*2 (1 lb.) loaves frozen Italian bread, thawed to room temperature*
*Olive oil*

Spray Long Loaf Pan with vegetable pan spray. Knead loaves together, let rest 15 minutes. Roll into oblong roll and place seam side down in pan. Clip with kitchen shears at three inch intervals, brush with olive oil. Let raise until doubled in size. Bake in 350°F preheated oven for 30 minutes or until browned and hollow sounding when tapped. Remove from pan and cool before slicing.

One loaf of bread will make 16-18 sandwiches. Paté or meat loaf will make approximately 25-30 servings as a sandwich or 45-50 appetizer servings.

*Why not serve picnic sandwiches with a dash of imagination instead of the same old cold cuts? Present these brimming paté sandwiches with all the trimmings — mustard, mayonnaise and chili sauce — to suit everyone's taste. The paté also makes a delicious appetizer, served in small slices with mustard, pickles and bread. The Wilton Long Loaf Pan is the perfect size for breads, meat loaves or cakes to serve a crowd.*

# Coconut Pineapple Cake With Cream Cheese Frosting

*Performance Pans™ 9 x 13 in. Sheet Pan*
*Wilton 9 x 13 in. Cake Cover*

***Cake:***
*2 cups all-purpose flour*
*2 teaspoons baking soda*
*½ teaspoon salt*
*¾ cup vegetable oil*
*¾ cup buttermilk*
*3 eggs*
*1 teaspoon Wilton Clear Vanilla*
*2 cups granulated sugar*
*1 (8 oz.) can crushed pineapple, drained*
*1½ cups coconut*

***Frosting:***
*Wilton Tip #10*
*Wilton Disposable Decorating Bags*
*3 cups sifted confectioners sugar*
*4 oz. cream cheese, softened*
*5 tablespoons butter*
*1 tablespoon milk*
*1½ cups toasted coconut*

Preheat oven to 350°F. Grease and flour Wilton 9 x 13 in. Sheet Pan. Mix flour, baking soda, and salt. In a separate bowl, whisk oil, buttermilk, eggs and vanilla. Add sugar, pineapple and coconut; mix well. Stir in flour mixture. Pour into prepared pan. Bake on center rack for 30-35 minutes or until an inserted cake tester comes out clean. Cool.

In a small bowl, combine all frosting ingredients. Beat until smooth. Spread over cooled cake. Garnish with toasted coconut if desired. To toast coconut, spread 1½ cups coconut on a cookie sheet, toast in a preheated 350°F oven for 3-5 minutes. Watch closely; coconut burns easily. This amount of frosting (2⅓ cups) will ice the top with a thin layer. Double amount of frosting if you wish to garnish with border or have a thicker layer of icing on cake. Pipe tip #10 bead border after adding toasted coconut.

Makes 16 servings.

*Perfect for picnics, the Wilton Cake Cover lets you bring along the dessert intact and keep it fresh for days. Designed to fit the 9 x 13 in. Performance Pan, this see-through cover lets everyone get their appetite set.*

# Little Loaves

*Wilton Mini Loaf Pan*
*1 (11 oz.) can refrigerator soft bread sticks, 8 sticks*
*Olive oil or melted butter*
*Sesame seeds, poppy seeds, caraway, garlic powder or Italian seasoning*

Preheat oven to 350°F. Spray Mini Loaf Pan with vegetable pan spray or brush with oil. Separate bread sticks into 4 pieces (two breadsticks each). Brush top with oil or butter, sprinkle with seasoning. Fold lengthwise, twist and place in pan. Bake for 20-25 minutes or until browned. Fill with your favorite sandwich fixings.

Makes 4 loaves.

# San Francisco Aspic

*Wilton 10½ in. Ring Mold Pan*
*6 cups tomato juice, divided*
*3 (3 oz.) packages lemon gelatin*
*1 tablespoon plus 1½ teaspoons lemon juice*
*1 teaspoon salt*
*1 tablespoon Worcestershire sauce*
*¾ cup chopped celery*
*¾ cup chopped sweet pickles*
*¾ cup diced cucumber*
*¾ cup chopped green pepper*
*¾ cup chopped pimento-stuffed green olives*
*½ cup grated onion*

This recipe comes from Judy Krasnow. Her mother, Ann Kailin, served it often.

Heat 2 cups tomato juice until boiling. Add gelatin and stir until completely dissolved. Add remaining tomato juice, lemon juice, salt and Worcestershire sauce. Set aside until slightly firm. Stir in chopped vegetables. Spray 10½ in. Ring Mold Pan with vegetable pan spray. Pour mixture into prepared pan. Chill 6 hours or overnight. To unmold, run thin bladed knife or spatula around outside and inside ring. Dip in hot water 2-3 seconds, unmold on serving platter. Garnish with cucumber slices and parsley, serve with thousand island dressing if desired.

Makes 12-16 servings.

*Little breads made in the Mini Loaf Pan are easy to pack for a Fourth of July picnic. They are best at room (or picnic spot) temperature. Fill them with your favorite sandwich filling—(we used roast beef and honey mustard), or serve plain loaves with a selection of cheese and fruit. Finish your picnic with a red, white and blue gelatin mold made in the Ring Mold Pan—just make layers of cherry and blueberry gelatin and lemon gelatin combined with whipped cream.*

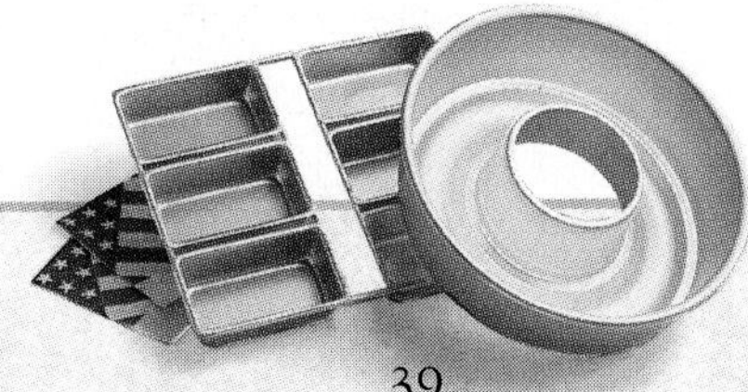

# Ball Park Sundaes

*Wilton Sports Ball Pan Set*
*Wilton Tip #4*
*Wilton Red-Red Icing Color*
*Wilton Disposable Decorating Bags*
*½ gallon vanilla ice cream*
*Chopped nuts*
*6 bananas*
*Chocolate syrup*
*Strawberry sauce*
*Maraschino cherries*
*Buttercream icing (see pg. 19)*

Line both halves of Sports Ball Pan with plastic wrap. Soften ice cream by stirring, do not melt. Pack ice cream into pan halves. Cover and freeze at least overnight. One to two hours before serving, unmold, unwrap flat top and press halves together. Place on serving platter. Using a prepared bag and tip #4, pipe stitching: pipe 2 slightly curving strings at center of ball, add diagonal strings on either side. Return to freezer until ready to serve. Surround with sundae fixings on serving dish.

Makes 8-10 servings.

# Number One Popcorn

*Wilton Numbers Pan Set*
*Wilton Baseball Mitt Icing Decorations*
*10 cups popped popcorn*
*1 (14 oz.) package colored Wilton Candy Melts™* in favorite team colors or use White Wilton Candy Melts and Wilton Candy Colors*

**Brand confectionery coating*

Line Number One Pan with plastic wrap, allow ends to come over edge of pan. Melt Candy Melts according to package directions. Reserve two or three wafers to melt later and attach Baseball Mitt decorations. In a large mixing bowl, mix Melts with popcorn. Immediately press into prepared pan. Let set 2-3 minutes, remove carefully and set aside. When molds are completely set, about one hour, unwrap and attach decorations. Rewrap, store at room temperature. May be made one day ahead.

Makes approximately 18-20 number ones.

*Throw a party saluting the wide world of sports with our Sports Ball Pan! Create easy-to-decorate cakes for all seasons — basketball, golf, tennis, soccer, bowling and more. Fun Wilton Icing Decorations and candles are available to round out your championship party theme!*

# Basketball Toss

*Wilton Nesting Round Cookie Cutters*
*Wilton Basketball Icing Decorations*
*5 oz. cheddar cheese, unsliced*
*5 oz. Monterrey Jack cheese, unsliced*
*4 oz. ham, unsliced*
*8 oz. rotini or other pasta, cooked*
*½ green pepper, chopped*
*3 green onions, chopped*
*⅓ cup light olive oil*
*2 tablespoons vinegar*
*¼ teaspoon salt*
*Pepper, basil, oregano, optional*

Slice cheeses and ham into ¼-inch slices. Cut with Nesting Round Cutter. Set 6-8 pieces aside for garnish. Chop leftover cheese and meat in ¼-inch cubes. Combine with pasta, green pepper and onion. In separate small bowl, combine oil, vinegar and seasonings; add to pasta and mix. Top with reserved cheese and ham cut-outs. Place Icing Decorations on napkins.

Makes 4 main dish servings.

# Chili-Cheese Muffins

*Wilton Mini Ball Pan*
*3 tablespoons butter or margarine*
*½ cup chopped onion*
*½ cup sun dried tomatoes, soaked 30 minutes in hot water, drained and chopped*
*3 cups all purpose flour*
*1 tablespoon baking powder*
*½ teaspoon basil*
*1 teaspoon salt*
*¼ teaspoon pepper*
*1½ cups milk*
*1 egg, slightly beaten*
*½ cup shredded mozzarella*
*1 (4 oz.) can chopped green chilies, drained*

Preheat oven to 350°F. Grease Mini Ball Pan, or spray with vegetable oil spray. Saute onion in butter until limp and transparent, not brown; set aside. Add tomatoes to onion and sauté for additional 2 minutes. Combine flour, baking powder, basil, salt and pepper in large mixing bowl. Add remaining ingredients, including onion/tomato mixture, stir until just moistened; do not overmix. Fold in green chilies. Divide batter evenly into Mini Ball Pan. Bake 30-35 minutes or until toothpick inserted in center comes out clean. Cool 5 minutes, remove from pan.

Makes 12 muffins.

*The Mini Ball Pan can field dozens of winning cake ideas for game day, including caps, baseballs, basketballs, faces in the crowd and more. Wilton Icing Decorations are available in many major sports for fast decorating against the clock!*

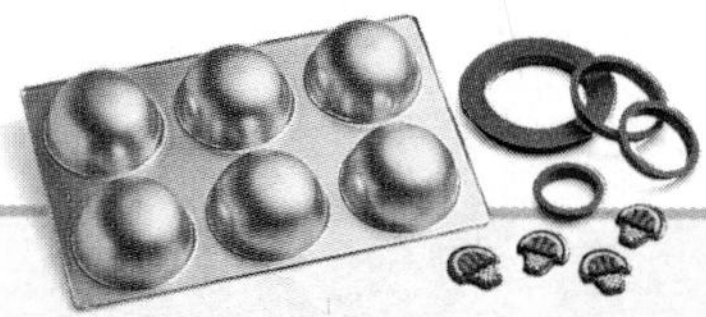

GO
TEAM!

# Football Hero

*Wilton First And Ten Football Pan*
*1 (16 oz.) loaf frozen Italian bread*
*½ cup mayonnaise*
*3 tablespoons prepared mustard*
*2 teaspoons horseradish (optional)*
*8 oz. sliced cheddar cheese*
*8 oz. sliced Fontina cheese*
*8 oz. sliced salami*
*8 oz. sliced turkey*
*8 oz. sliced ham*
*Leaf lettuce*
*Sliced onions*
*Sliced tomatoes*

Thaw frozen bread in refrigerator overnight or at room temperature. Spray Football Pan with vegetable pan spray. Place bread in pan, let raise 1½-2 hours or until doubled. Preheat oven to 350°F. To make loaf flat on bottom: place cookie sheet on top of pan and weigh down using heavy pan with oven proof handle. Bake 20 minutes, remove weight and cookie sheet. Bake an additional 5-10 minutes or until browned. Cool 5 minutes, remove from pan and cool completely. Split, spread with mayonnaise and mustard. Place cheese and meat in overlapping slices on bottom half of bread. Add lettuce, tomatoes and onions and top half of bread; press lightly and wrap in plastic wrap or foil. May be refrigerated one hour before serving. To serve, slice in 1-1½ in. slices.

Makes 6-8 servings.

*You can be confident of Wilton quality — our anodized aluminum pans, like the First And Ten Football Pan, produce perfectly defined baked goods that release with every detail intact. And, if you're serving a large party, add another football hero using our Handsome Guy Pan. Decorating instructions are on the label.*

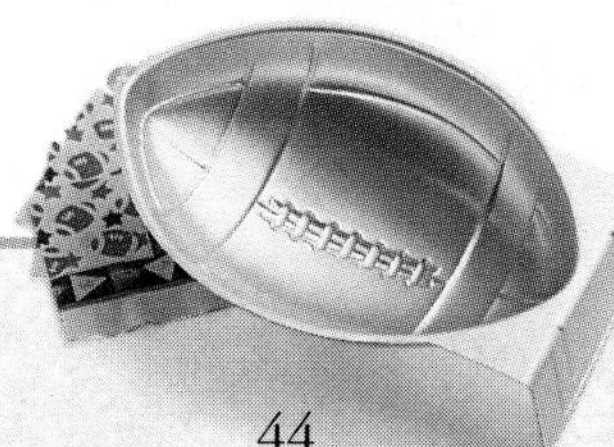

CHRIS
JACK

## 3-Ring Celebration

*At this birthday circus, a personal clown cookie greets every kid atop a chewy, crispy marshmallow treat. But our bright clown cake will be the main event—raising a cookie banner which declares your birthday boy or girl the star of the day.*

## Dinosaur Party

*It's a Jurassic classic, with cold cut sandwiches in favorite dino shapes, plus a gigantic filled peanut butter creme cookie to delight every kid in its path!*

## Teen Fiesta

*It's one spicy party when you serve individual taco salads filled with meat, cheese and vegetables. Next, think Mexican chilly—a giant ice cream "taco salad" to match, with fruit and candy toppings and a ladyfinger shell!*

## Ladies' Lunch

*Your guests will ask where you got these unique recipes: the Italian torta is a tempting beef, spinach and cheese pie in a tender crust; our ice cream and meringue cake makes a fantastic finish, wrapped in a flowing candy clay ribbon.*

## Wild West

*A hearty chili and cornbread supper, spurred to new frontiers by crunchy cracker shapes that take you back to the Old West. Round up the same fun shapes for the easy-to-make candies which decorate our luscious fudge layer cake.*

# BEST CLOWN IN TOWN!

*Wilton Cute Clown Pan*
*Wilton Alphabet Cookie Cutters*
*Wilton Tips 3, 16, 22, 125, 127D*
*Wilton Lemon Yellow, Royal Blue, Christmas Red Icing Colors*
*Wilton Cake Board, Fanci-Foil Wrap*
*Roll-Out Cookie Dough Recipe*
*Buttercream Icing (see pg. 19)*
*Black string licorice, candy wafers, large gumball, candy corn*

NOTE: For instructions or specific decorating techniques, see the current Wilton Yearbook of Cake Decorating.

Using Roll-Out Cookie Dough recipe (see below) and Alphabet Cookie Cutters, cut desired letters. Bake and cool. Using buttercream icing, outline cookies with tip 3, then fill in with tip 16 stars. Set aside.

Bake a two-layer cake mix in Wilton Cute Clown Pan, cool. Ice smooth: face area in white, hair in yellow. Using tip 3 pipe mouth, eyes and eyebrows. Using tip 22, cover hat with stars, add zigzag brim. Outline inside arm area using tip 3; cover suit with tip 22 stars, add tip 3 dots. Cover hands and feet with tip 22 stars. Add tip 125 ruffle at cuffs and ankles; tip 127D ruffle at neck. Add candy corn for hair, candy wafers for cheeks, large gumball for nose. Position cookies and black string licorice.

Makes 12 servings.

# TAKE HOME TREATS

***Crispy Cereal Stands***
*Wilton Mini Angel Food Pan*
*1/4 cup (1/2 stick) margarine*
*1 (10 oz.) package (approximately 40) regular marshmallows*
*6 1/2 cups crispy rice cereal*
*Butter for pans and hands*
*Candy coated chocolate bits*
*Clown cookies*

Melt margarine in large saucepan over low heat; add marshmallows and stir until completely melted. Remove from heat and add cereal, stir until coated. Butter Mini Angel Food Pans, pack mixture into pans with buttered hands. Remove by running a small spatula around edge of pan. Press on candies while stands are sticky. When set (2-3 hours) make slots with spatula for cookies to stand. Press decorated cookies into slots. If necessary, prop from back with craft stick.

***Roll-Out Cookie Recipe***
*Wilton Clown Cookie Cutter*
*Wilton Tip #3*
*1 cup butter or margarine, softened*
*1 cup sugar*
*1 large egg*
*1 teaspoon Wilton Clear Vanilla*
*2 teaspoons baking powder*
*3 cups flour*
*Buttercream Icing (see pg. 19)*

Preheat oven to 400°F. In a large bowl, cream butter and sugar with an electric mixer. Beat in eggs and vanilla. Add baking powder and flour one cup at a time, mixing after each addition. The dough will be very stiff; blend last flour in by hand. Do not chill dough. Divide dough into 2 balls. On a floured surface, roll each ball in a circle approximately 12 in. in diameter and 1/8 in. thick. Dip cutters in flour before each use. Bake cookies on ungreased cookie sheet on middle rack of oven for 6 to 10 minutes, or until cookies are lightly browned. Cool completely, at least 3 hours. Decorate with tip 3 lines, dots and zigzags. Add tip 3 name.

*Clowns are an all-time kids' favorite—so why not create a 3-ring circus of party treats? It's easy with Wilton pans, cutters, icing decorations, cake tops and baking cups in colorful clown designs!*

LIZZIE
DAN
MEG
CHRIS

# Peanut Butter Dino Sandwich Cookie

*Wilton Partysaurus Pan*

***Cookie:***
*1 cup solid vegetable shortening*
*1 cup peanut butter*
*1 cup granulated sugar*
*1 cup packed brown sugar*
*2 eggs*
*1 teaspoon Wilton Clear Vanilla*
*3 cups flour*
*1 teaspoon baking soda*
*Dash salt*

***Filling:***
*1 (16 oz.) jar marshmallow creme*

***Chocolate Piping:***
*Wilton Disposable Decorating Bags*
*1 cup chocolate chips*
*1 tablespoon butter*

Preheat oven to 350°F. Grease and flour Partysaurus Pan. In a large mixing bowl, cream together shortening and peanut butter. Gradually add sugars, blending well. Add eggs, one at a time, beating until smooth. Add vanilla. Set aside. Combine flour, baking soda and salt. Stir into peanut butter mixture. Divide dough into two parts. Wrap and refrigerate one hour or overnight. Press one part into prepared pan. Bake 20 minutes or until lightly browned. Cool 5 minutes, run a small flexible spatula around edge, release and cool on rack. Bake remaining dough in the same way. To assemble, place one cookie on serving plate embossed side up. Spread with marshmallow creme. Place second cookie on top, press lightly.

Melt chocolate chips and butter together on low heat in microwave or top of range. Fill Decorating Bag with melted chocolate, clip end. Pipe chocolate onto cookie.

Makes 16-20 servings.

# Mini Dinosaur Sandwiches

*Wilton Mini Dinosaur Pan*
*1 (16 oz.) pkg. hot roll mix*
*12 (1 oz.) slices cheese*
*2 lbs. lunchmeat*
*Lettuce*
*Tomatoes*

Prepare hot roll mix according to package directions, up to shaping rolls. Divide dough into 12 equal pieces*. Grease Mini Dinosaur Pan with solid vegetable shortening or use a vegetable pan spray. Form dough into flat oblongs and press into pan; the surface of dough toward bottom of pan should be very smooth. Cover and let rise in warm place until doubled in bulk, approximately 30 minutes. Bake at 375°F for 15-20 minutes or until browned. Cool 5 minutes in pan and remove to rack to cool.

When dino rolls are cool, split and top with lunchmeat, cheese, lettuce and tomato. Makes 12 sandwiches.

*If using one pan, refrigerate 6 pieces of dough until first six have baked. Then follow directions for rising and baking.

*Plan your party theme and invite Wilton...we'll coordinate the celebration from start to finish! A wide variety of matching Wilton products are available in everything from shaped bakeware to cookie cutters, candy molds, cupcake papers and candles.*

CD PLAYER
SONY
DDD

# Individual Taco Salads

*Wilton Jumbo Muffin Pans*
*1 lb. ground beef*
*½ medium onion, chopped*
*1 (1.25 oz.) package taco seasoning mix*
*1 (15 oz.) can tomato sauce*
*6 large flour tortillas*

***Garnish:***
*Shredded lettuce*
*Chopped tomatoes*
*Chopped avocado*
*Sour cream*
*Cilantro*

In a large skillet, break up ground beef with fork, brown, pour off fat. Add onion and sauté 3-4 minutes, add taco mix and tomato sauce. Simmer 10-15 minutes or until thick.

For shells: Preheat oven to 400°F. Soften 6 tortillas 1-2 minutes in microwave. Place over back of jumbo muffin pan. Softened tortillas will fold around pan. Place another muffin pan over shells, press lightly. Bake 7-8 minutes or until crisp. Remove and cool. Fill with meat mixture and garnishes.

Makes 6 salads.

# "Taco" Ice Cream Dessert

*Wilton 9 in. Springform Pan*
*Wilton Kelly Green, Orange Icing Color*
*Wilton Tip #352*
*1 (4 dozen ct.) package lady fingers*
*½ gallon of ice cream*
*¼ cup shaved chocolate*
*½ cup chopped sweetened strawberries*
*½ cup shredded coconut*
*½ cup Buttercream Icing tinted green (see pg. 19)*
*1 cup frozen whipped topping or whipped cream*

Place ladyfingers, rounded side out, around edge and on bottom of 9 in. Springform Pan. Soften ice cream by stirring, do not melt, pack into pan. Cover & freeze. Remove from springform before decorating. To tint coconut, place shredded coconut in plastic sandwich bag. Add a few drops of Wilton Orange Icing Color (diluted slightly with water). Shake bag until color is evenly distributed. When ready to serve, garnish with chocolate, strawberries, whipped cream and tinted coconut to resemble taco salad. Randomly pipe #352 lettuce leaves in buttercream.

*Muffins come in all sizes at Wilton! From brunch-size mini muffins to standard cupcake-size to jumbo and popover style, Wilton has the muffin pan you need to make them all. You'll find excellent Wilton kitchen-tested muffin recipes on each label.*

# Italian Torta

*Wilton 9 in. Springform Pan*
*1 package (16 oz.) hot roll mix*
*1 lb. ground beef*
*½ medium onion, chopped*
*1 clove garlic, minced*
*1 teaspoon oregano*
*½ teaspoon basil*
*½ cup water*
*1 can (6 oz.) tomato paste*
*1 package (10 oz.) frozen chopped spinach, thawed*
*1 cup ricotta or cottage cheese, drained*
*Salt and pepper to taste*
*1 cup mozzarella cheese, shredded*
*1 egg, beaten*

Prepare hot roll mix according to package directions. While dough is rising, brown ground beef and onion; drain fat. Add seasonings, water and tomato paste. Squeeze excess moisture from spinach and combine with ricotta cheese. Salt and pepper to taste. After fillings are prepared, divide dough into 3 portions and roll each into a 9 in. circle. Fit one portion into a buttered 9 in. Springform Pan. Spread meat almost to edges of dough. Sprinkle mozzarella cheese on top of meat. Add next layer of dough and allow to rise 10 minutes. Spread with spinach mixture. Place remaining dough on top and cover with damp cloth. Set pan in warm place and allow to rise about 40 minutes. When doubled in size, score top with sharp knife into 8 pie shaped wedges. Brush top with egg. Bake on lower oven rack at 350°F for 40-50 minutes or until crust is golden brown. Let set 15 minutes before slicing.

Makes 8 servings.

*Wilton Springform Pans provide the support and even heating needed for dense meat pies and cheesecakes. They'll heat thoroughly to the center, yet won't burn a delicate crust. And Springform Pans make it easy to remove and serve entreés and desserts which cannot be inverted. Available in anodized aluminum and non-stick.*

# Nut Meringue With Caramel Ice Cream

*Wilton 9 in. Round Pans*
*Wilton Leaf Green Icing Color*
*Wilton Tips 3, 21, 2110*
*Whipping Cream*
*Buttercream icing (see pg. 19)*

***Meringue***
*2 tablespoons Wilton Meringue Powder*
*½ cup cold water*
*¾ cup plus 1 tablespoon sugar*
*1 cup finely chopped pecans*

***Filling***
*2 quarts softened vanilla ice cream*
*1 cup prepared caramel sauce, divided*

***Icing***
*2 cups whipping cream, whipped with ¼ cup sugar and 1 teaspoon vanilla (see pg. 72)*

***Candy Clay Bow***
*Wilton Candy Melts™* (1 bag Pink needed)*
*⅓ cup light corn syrup*
**brand confectionery coating*

NOTE: This meringue recipe was made twice. Do not double meringue recipe. *Make it two times.*

Preheat oven to 275°F. Make four meringue layers. Butter two 9 in. round pans. In a large mixing bowl, combine meringue powder, water and 6 tablespoons of the sugar. Beat at high speed for 5 minutes. Gradually add remaining sugar and continue beating at high speed for 5 minutes until meringue is stiff and dry. Fold in pecans. Spread in prepared pans. Bake 1 hour; turn oven off and leave meringue in oven for 1 hour. Remove meringue from pans by loosening with sharp knife. Cool, repeat for remaining two meringue layers.

Make four ice cream layers. Line 9 in. round pans with foil. Use enough to fold over top of ice cream to store in freezer. Divide in fourths softened ice cream, spoon into prepared pans. Swirl ¼ cup of caramel sauce into each pan with ice cream. Freeze until firm, cover. Remove from pan and store until needed.

To assemble, place meringue on serving plate. Unmold ice cream; remove foil. Place on top of meringue. Repeat layering process.

To make ahead, assemble meringue and ice cream. Freeze assembled meringue and ice cream *only* one day ahead. When ready to serve, frost with whipped cream. Pipe tip 21 top and tip 2110 bottom shell borders, add tip 3 message. Iced cake can be replaced in the freezer 1-2 hours before serving. Place Candy Clay bow and ribbon on at serving time. Makes 20 servings.

***Candy Clay Bow:***
Melt candy as directed on package. Stir in corn syrup and mix only until blended. Shape mixture into a 6 in. square on waxed paper and let set at room temperature until dry. Wrap well and store at room temperature until needed. Candy clay handles best if hardened overnight. Several days in advance, roll out candy clay to approx ⅛ in. thick; sprinkle surface with cornstarch to prevent sticking. Cut the following pieces, all ¾ in. wide and approx. 7 in. long: six bow loops, four streamers with ends trimmed into "v". After trimming, shape into bow and let set on sides. Shape streamers as shown, position on crumpled foil or waxed paper to add dimension and let set.

***Candy Clay for Chocolate Walnut Honor Roll (shown on pg. 25)***
Prepare Candy Clay as above, using RED Candy Melts, and cutting the following pieces, ¾ in. wide: two bow loops about 7 in. long; one loop for center of bow about 3 in. long; two streamers about 6 in. long, with end trimmed into "v". After trimming, shape into bow and wave-shaped streamers as shown; place on side edge to set. On day of party, cut a strip ¾ in. wide to fit around cake.

*Wilton Round Pans, sized from 6 in. to 18 in., are indispensable for entertaining!*

You look great for your age.
Where's the CAKE?!
Happy Birthday! Ann

## *Man's Birthday*

# TEXAS CHILI

*1 large dried mild Ancho chili pepper*
*1 lb. ground sirloin*
*1 medium onion, cut in 4-5 pieces*
*1 garlic clove, cut in 4-5 pieces*
*1 tablespoon chili powder*
*1 teaspoon cumin*
*1 can (28 oz.) peeled plum tomatoes, drained*
*1 (15 oz.) can red kidney beans, undrained*
*1 (4 oz.) can chopped green chilies, undrained*
*½ teaspoon salt*

Roast dried chili pepper in hot skillet until lightly browned. Split, remove seeds and soak in 2¼ cups hot water. In large heavy saucepan (2 qt.) sauté sirloin, do not brown. Break up chunks with wooden spoon. Fit food processor with metal blade. Add onion and garlic. Process 10-12 turns or until finely chopped; add to meat along with chili powder and cumin; sauté until tender. Place tomatoes and chili pepper with water into processor. Process until most chunks are broken up. Add to meat mixture. Add beans, canned chilies and salt. Simmer 15 minutes; taste and add more chili powder if desired. Simmer an additional hour.

Serve garnished with sour cream, chopped onions and cilantro.

Makes 4 one-cup servings.

# CORNMEAL CRACKERS

*Wilton 5-Pc. Bite-Size Western Cookie Cutter Set*
*1 cup flour*
*½ cup yellow cornmeal*
*¼ teaspoon salt*
*2 oz. cold butter (½ stick)*
*2½ oz. cold cream cheese*
*1 tablespoon cold water*
*Onion powder, chili powder or garlic salt to taste*

Preheat oven to 400°F. In bowl of food processor fitted with metal blade, process flour, cornmeal and salt with 3-4 short pulses. With machine running add pieces of butter and cream cheese one at a time. Stop machine; add tablespoon of cold water. Process until dough just holds together. Form into ball, chill 30 minutes, roll ⅛ in. thick. Cut out with Bite-Size Western Cookie Cutters. Sprinkle with either onion powder, chili powder, or garlic salt before baking. Bake for 10-12 minutes. Cool, store in airtight container.

Makes approximately 4 dozen crackers.

# CORN LOAVES

*Wilton Mini-Loaf Pan*
*1 cup flour*
*1 cup cornmeal*
*3 tablespoons sugar*
*4 teaspoons baking powder*
*1 teaspoon salt*
*1 cup milk*
*¼ cup oil*
*1 egg, slightly beaten*
*1 (11 oz.) can Mexican-style corn, well drained*
*1 (4 oz.) can green chilies*
*2 teaspoons finely chopped jalapeños*

Heat oven to 400°F. Spray Mini-Loaf Pan with non-stick vegetable oil. In medium bowl, combine first 5 ingredients. Stir in milk, oil and egg, beat just until smooth. Fold in corn, chilies, and jalapeños and pour batter into prepared pan. Bake 15 minutes or until brown. Cool 5 minutes, remove from pan. Makes 6 loaves.

*Wilton Cookie Cutters aren't just for fun cookie-making! Add spice to any party with appetizers or sandwiches cut in appropriate shapes — we have everything from dinosaurs to dogs, baby bottles to boats.*

# Chocolate-Chocolate Layer Cake

*Wilton 8-in. or 9-in. Round Cake Pans*
*Wilton Gold Jumbo Candles*
*6 squares semi-sweet chocolate*
*¾ cup (1½ sticks) butter or margarine*
*1½ cups sugar*
*3 eggs*
*2 teaspoons Wilton Clear Vanilla*
*2½ cups all-purpose flour, divided*
*1 teaspoon baking soda*
*½ teaspoon salt*
*1½ cups water*

Preheat oven to 350°F. Grease and flour two 8-in. or 9-in. round pans.

Microwave chocolate and butter in large microwaveable bowl at HIGH 2 minutes (or until butter is melted) or melt on top of range in heavy saucepan over low heat. Stir until chocolate is completely melted.

Stir sugar into melted chocolate mixture until well blended. With electric mixer at low speed, beat in eggs, one at time, until completely mixed. Add vanilla. Stir in ½ cup of the flour, the baking soda and the salt. Beat in remaining flour alternately with water until well blended and smooth.

Pour into prepared pans. Bake for 30-35 minutes or until cake tests done. Cool in pan 10 minutes. Remove and cool completely. Ice with Silky Chocolate Buttercream. Top with Western candies and candles.

### *Silky Chocolate Buttercream Icing*

*4 egg yolks*
*1½ cups confectioners sugar*
*1 cup (2 sticks) butter, in 16 pieces (room temperature)*
*2 teaspoons Wilton Clear Vanilla*
*2 oz. unsweetened chocolate, melted*

Combine egg yolks and sugar in medium mixing bowl, beat on medium speed until pale and thick. Add ½ of butter, beat until smooth, add remaining butter 1 piece at a time, beating after each addition. Add vanilla and melted chocolate, beat until blended.

### *Wild West Candies*

*1 (14 oz.) bag Wilton Candy Melts,™* White*
*Wilton Jelly Roll/Cookie Pan*
*Wilton 5-Pc. Bite-Size Western Cookie Cutter Set*
**Brand confectionery coating*

Follow package directions for melting Candy Melts in microwave. Pour melted Candy Melts in an even layer on Jelly Roll/Cookie Pan. Let set partially, about 5 minutes, then cut shapes with Cookie Cutters. Let candy set until hard, then lift shapes away from pan. Place candies on cake as shown.

*You can make a plain cake come to life with Wilton Cookie Cutters! For a fast way to decorate, just imprint your favorite cutter designs on top of your smooth iced cake. Outline the marked design then fill-in with stars in any color you like.*

SHERIFF
JACK
SHERIFF

# Holidays

## Valentine's Day

*Desserts to get passionate about . . . a sumptuous strawberry shortcake made with flaky heart pastry wafers and our chocolate-drizzled meringue-macadamia torte.*

## Easter

*Fresh looks and tastes of spring: A fragrant rosemary and raisin bread made in our Little Lamb Pan, tangy egg-shaped lemon tarts plus bunny shortbreads and a giant egg pound cake, layered with refreshing orange sherbet.*

## Halloween

*Jack O'Lantern appears in many delicious disguises . . . pumpkin cookies oozing with raisins, candy-coated mini shortbreads, a pumpkin cake iced in maple buttercream and petite pumpkin brownies on a bed of chocolate dirt. Be very afraid!*

## Thanksgiving

*Twists on tradition create a meal to remember. Guests will give thanks for the tart taste of our swirled cranberry salad, the light, springy texture of pumpkin bread pudding, the velvety richness of brandy chocolate pecan pie and sweet potato pie.*

## Christmas

*Make merry with a party buffet featuring all the trimmings. Begin the seaon's feasting with a chicken-artichoke mousse molded in our Treeliteful Pan. Festively decorated spritz cookies, cherry tarts and a glazed banana-ginger fruitcake capture the holiday spirit.*

## New Year's Eve

*Perfect partners with champagne: zesty blue cheese spread molded in our Viennese Swirl Pan, served with fruit and crackers . . . plus, the Grand Finale—a decadent chocolate truffle dessert on a pool of raspberry sauce. Two dazzling ways to toast a year of wonderful celebrations!*

# Strawberry Heart Towers

*Wilton 6-Piece Nesting Heart Cookie Cutter Set*
*Even-Bake® Insulated Cookie Sheets*

***Pastry***
*2¼ cups flour*
*1 teaspoon salt*
*½ cup cold butter*
*¼ cup shortening*
*5-6 tablespoons cold water*

***Topping***
*2 tablespoons sugar*
*1 tablespoon cinnamon*

***Filling***
*1 quart strawberries, sliced, mix with 2 tablespoons sugar or to taste*
*1 cup whipping cream, whipped*

***Caramel Cage***
*⅔ cup granulated sugar*
*¼ cup light corn syrup*
*⅓ cup water*

Preheat oven to 425°F. Combine flour and salt in bowl or in work bowl of food processor fitted with metal blade. Cut shortening and butter into flour with pastry blender or on/off pulses of food processor until mixture resembles coarse meal. Add water a few tablespoons at a time until dough just holds together. Form into two flat disks and refrigerate at least 30 minutes. Roll on lightly floured surface to ⅛ in. thickness. Starting with smallest heart cut 5 nesting sizes for each dessert. Place on cookie sheet (for even baking, bake all small hearts on one cookie sheet), sprinkle with cinnamon and sugar. Reroll for remaining hearts. Bake for 5-10 minutes or until lightly browned. Remove and cool. Pastry can be baked one day ahead and stored in airtight container. Layer pastry with sweetened berries and whipped cream.

Makes 6 desserts.

***To Make Caramel Cage:***
Read all the instructions for this recipe before beginning.

Place sugar, syrup and water in small heavy saucepan, stir and blend ingredients. Place on high heat and cook until syrup turns a light amber. Do not stir, wash the sides of the pan down with a pastry brush dipped in hot water about every 2 minutes. It will take 7-9 minutes for mixture to cook. Watch closely at the end; sugar can burn easily. When light amber, remove from heat, wait for bubbles to disappear (3-4 minutes), dip tines of fork in syrup and pull up. Caramel threads will form. Twirl around shortcakes. If threads do not form, wait a few minutes until syrup cools slightly. Syrup can be reheated carefully over low heat.

Caramel cages can be added 10-15 minutes before serving. To clean utensils, soak in hot water or fill pan with water and bring to boil.

*Wilton Nesting Cutter Sets are a great idea. They give you the most popular cookie-baking shapes — hearts, rounds, stars and bears — in 6 popular sizes. Make a triple-decker sandwich cookie, a bear cookie family or star designs traced in icing on a birthday cake. Use your imagination!*

# Chocolate Meringue Macadamia Torte

*Wilton 9 in. Heart Pans*
*1 Roll Wilton Parchment*
*Wilton tip #2110*

***Chocolate Filling:***
*8 ounces sweet baking chocolate*
*3 tablespoons confectioners sugar*
*3 tablespoons coffee-flavored liqueur*
*4 egg yolks, beaten*
*4 egg whites*
*1 cup whipping cream, whipped*
*1½ cups chopped macadamia nuts*
*Chocolate dipped macadamia nuts, whipped cream, melted chocolate for garnish*

***Chocolate Meringue:***
*2 tablespoons Wilton Meringue Powder*
*½ cup cold water*
*¾ cup plus 1 tablespoon granulated sugar*
*4 tablespoons unsweetened cocoa*

***To Make Filling:***
Melt chocolate over hot, not boiling water in double boiler. Combine confectioners sugar, liqueur and egg yolks. Stir into chocolate. Cook over medium heat, stirring constantly with whisk until mixture is warm and thickened (about 6 minutes). Cool. Beat egg whites until stiff peaks form. Stir into cooled chocolate mixture. Fold in whipped cream until well blended. Fold in ½ cup chopped nuts; reserve remaining nuts for assembling torte. Cover and chill filling until ready to serve torte (at least 1 hour).

***To Make Meringues:***
You will need to make four meringue layers. If you have four pans, bake at one time; if you are using two pans, repeat instructions for two more layers.

Preheat oven to 300°F. Grease two Heart Pans, cut parchment and fit into bottom of pans. In a large bowl, combine Meringue Powder, water, cocoa and ½ cup sugar. Whip at high speed for 5 minutes. Gradually add remaining sugar and continue whipping at high speed for 5 minutes until meringue is stiff and dry. Place approximately 1½ cups meringue mixture in prepared pans and spread evenly. Cover bowl with damp cloth and reserve remaining mixture for two more meringues. Bake at 300°F for 1 hour or until meringue is set and dry. Cool 30 minutes. Remove from pans, invert and remove parchment. Rewhip reserved meringue and follow above instructions to bake two additional layers. Baked and cooled meringue layers can be stored 1-2 days in an airtight container in a cool, dry place.

***To Assemble Torte:***
Just before serving, spread ⅓ of filling on each of three meringue layers. Sprinkle with ¼ cup chopped macadamia nuts. Stack filled layers atop each other on serving plate. Top with fourth meringue layer. Garnish with tip #2110 whipped cream rosettes and chocolate dipped macadamia nuts; drizzle melted chocolate over top. Can be assembled 30-45 minutes before serving. To cut, use a serrated knife in a sawing motion. Makes 18-20 servings.

*Create any romantic dessert your heart desires with the wide variety of Wilton Heart Pans. Unveil an elaborate stacked heart cake using the Heart Pan Set, or surprise your family with delightful bite-size muffins or brownies made in our Petite Heart Pan.*

# Rosemary Fruit Bread

*Wilton Little Lamb Pan Set*
*Wilton Tips 3, 16*
*Wilton Violet, Daffodil Yellow Icing Colors*
*Wilton Meringue Powder*
*4-4½ cups all purpose flour*
*⅓ cup sugar*
*½ teaspoon salt*
*1 package fast-rising yeast*
*5 tablespoons butter, cut into small pieces*
*½ teaspoon crushed rosemary*
*1⅓ cups hot water (120-130°F)*
*1 egg*
*½ cup diced dried fruit bits*
*Royal Icing (see recipe on Meringue Powder can)*
*Fresh rosemary for necklace*

Grease front and back sections of Little Lamb Pan. In large bowl, combine 2 cups flour, sugar, salt, yeast, butter and rosemary. Gradually add hot water, stirring to melt butter. Add egg; beat well. Stir in dried fruit bits and enough remaining flour to make a soft dough. Knead dough on lightly floured surface 8 to 10 minutes, or until smooth and elastic. Place in back of prepared pan; tie top of pan over bottom with string. Let dough rise 30 minutes, or until doubled in size. Preheat oven to 350°F. Bake bread 35 to 40 minutes or until lightly browned. Remove from mold and cool. Serve with butter curls, made with butter curler.

Make swirled drop flowers for necklace, using royal icing and tip 16. Hold decorating bag at a 90° angle, with tip touching work surface. Curve wrist around to the left, and as you squeeze out icing, bring hand back to the right. Stop pressure, pull tip away. Add tip 3 dot center. Let dry. To make necklace, use a 10 to 12 in. stem of fresh rosemary. Fasten ends with twine. Attach drop flowers with a dot of royal icing.

Makes 12 to 14 servings.

*Use the Little Lamb Pan Set to create a beautiful cake centerpiece for your Easter table. Fluff up his wool coat, using a spatula to swirl on buttercream icing, add dot eyes and a drop flower necklace. Your lamb can rest in a bed of tinted green coconut.*

# Lemon Mousse Tarts

*Wilton Petite Egg Pan*
*Wilton Tip #21*
*Wilton Disposable Decorating Bags*
*Wilton Meringue Powder*
*1 package unflavored gelatin*
*¾ cup fresh lemon juice, divided (3-4 lemons)*
*4 egg yolks*
*1 cup sugar*
*Grated rind of one lemon*
*1½ cups whipping cream, whipped to soft peaks*
*1 recipe, Basic Pastry Crust (see pg. 87)*
*Royal Icing (follow instructions on Meringue Powder label)*

Soften gelatin in ¼ cup lemon juice, set aside. In small heavy saucepan, lightly beat eggs, add sugar and remaining ½ cup lemon juice and mix. Cook over low heat, stirring constantly 5-8 minutes or until thickened and mixture coats a metal spoon. Add lemon rind and softened gelatin. Cool until thick, then whisk over pan of cold water. Add approximately ¼ cup whipped cream to lemon mixture to lighten, fold lemon mixture into whipped cream.

Make Basic Pastry Crust recipe, following instructions on pg. 87, up to forming and rolling of dough. Form pastry into small balls, press into Petite Egg Pan, prick with fork. Bake at 375°F for 7-10 minutes. Cool 5 minutes, remove and cool. Using tip #21 and Disposable Decorating Bag, pipe lemon mousse into pastry shells. Following directions on pg. 68, make Royal Icing swirled drop flowers to top each shell.

Makes 4 dozen eggs.

# Shortbread Bunnies

*Wilton Mini Bunny Pan*
*1 cup butter*
*¾ cup sugar*
*1 teaspoon Wilton Clear Vanilla*
*2½ cups flour*
*Ribbon*

In a medium mixing bowl cream butter, sugar and vanilla. Add flour and mix until dough is smooth. Chill dough one hour.

Preheat oven to 300°F. Spray Mini Bunny Pan with vegetable pan spray. Press dough in pan. Bake 15-20 minutes, or until very lightly browned. Cool 10 minutes in pans, then remove bunnies to cool. Tie on a ribbon bow before serving. Shortbread can be stored in an airtight container at room temperature for several weeks or frozen for two months.

Makes 12 bunnies.

*After everyone has colored their eggs, let them decorate their own little Easter cakes! The Mini Bunny and Petite Egg Pans are just the right size for kids to get creative. They can go wild with their favorite faces, colors and designs!*

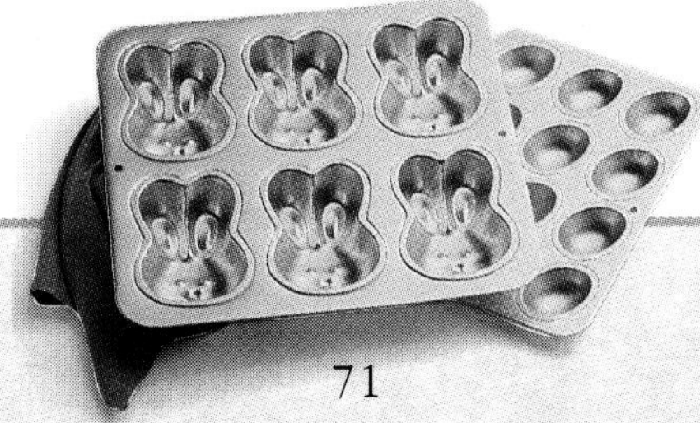

# Sherbet Egg Poundcake

*Wilton 3-D Egg Pan Set*
*Wilton Leaf Green, Violet Icing Colors*
*1½ cups butter*
*2½ cups sugar*
*5 eggs*
*3 cups all-purpose flour*
*¾ teaspoon baking powder*
*¼ teaspoon salt*
*1 cup milk*
*1 teaspoon Wilton Clear Vanilla Extract*
*¾ teaspoon Wilton Almond Extract*
*1 quart orange sherbet*
*2 cups (16 oz.) whipping cream, whipped with 3 tablespoons sugar or use 2 cups (16 oz.) non-dairy whipping product, whipped*
*Shredded coconut*
*Orange peel for garnish*

Preheat oven to 325°F. Grease and flour each half of 3-D Egg Pan. Ingredients should be at room temperature. Cream butter and sugar until light and fluffy. Add eggs one at a time, mixing well between each addition. Sift flour with baking powder and salt. Add flour mixture alternately with milk; add flour first. Mix in Vanilla and Almond Extract. Pour into prepared pans and bake for approximately 1 hour or until cake tests done. Cool 10 minutes. Remove from pan, slice off any crown and cool egg halves flat side down. When completely cool, slice each half in three horizontal layers. Soften 1 quart of orange sherbet. Line each egg pan half with plastic wrap. Starting with cake in bottom, layer with cake and sherbet. Wrap and freeze overnight. Remove and ice with whipped cream. The non-dairy cream available in 8 oz. cartons whips and holds its shape well — or use regular whipped cream. Do not use frozen whipped topping.

***To whip cream:***
Have bowl, cream and beaters very cold. Add sugar and whip at medium speed until stiff. Do not overbeat or cream will be coarse and difficult to spread.

***To paint designs:***
Thin 1 teaspoon of each Wilton Icing Color with a few drops of water. Use a medium size good quality paint brush to paint designs. Brush lightly on icing.

Tint coconut green, following directions on pg. 53. Place egg cake on bed of coconut.

***To make orange peel garnish:***
Using a citrus stripper, make one long length of peel. Tie in bow, wrap ends around a pencil or chop stick. Refrigerate and cover with damp cloth until ready to use.

Makes two cakes and 12-14 servings.

*The 3-D Egg Pan Set makes so many colorful Easter centerpieces. This two-pan set includes instructions for 5 designs — from a quick-iced egg cake to an intricate floral masterpiece. And you'll love the molded chocolate egg design, ideal for decorating and filling with Easter candy!*

# Raisin Filled Pumpkin Cookies

*Wilton 4-Pc. Jack-O-Lantern Cookie Cutter Set*
*Wilton Orange Icing Color*
*1 cup butter*
*1 cup sugar*
*1 large egg*
*1 teaspoon Wilton Clear Vanilla*
*2 teaspoons baking powder*
*1 tablespoon pumpkin pie spice*
*2¾ cups flour*

***Filling***
*2 cups raisins*
*¾ cup chopped walnuts*
*½ cup frozen orange juice concentrate thawed, undiluted*

Preheat oven to 375°F. In large bowl, cream butter and sugar with an electric mixer. Beat in egg and vanilla. Add baking powder, spice and flour, one cup at a time, mixing after each addition. The dough will be very stiff; blend last flour in by hand. Do not chill dough. To tint with icing color, add small amounts until desired color is reached.

Divide dough into 2 balls. On a floured surface, roll each ball into a circle approximately 12 inches in diameter. Cut pumpkin shapes, dipping cutters in flour before each use. Place half the cookies on cookie sheets. Mix all filling ingredients in small bowl. Or fill with a layer of jelly. Place 1 tablespoon filling on cookie. Cut eyes and mouth from remaining cookies. Place on top of filling. Press to seal edges. Bake for 12-15 minutes or until lightly browned.

Makes 12 cookies.

# Mini Pumpkin Shortbreads

*Wilton Petite Pumpkin Pan*
*Wilton Orange Icing Color*
*1 (14 oz.) pkg. Wilton Candy Melts™*, Dark Cocoa*
*Wilton Disposable Decorating Bag*
*Wilton Decorator Brush Set*
*1 cup butter*
*¾ cup sugar*
*1 teaspoon Wilton Clear Vanilla*
*2½ cups flour*
**Brand confectionery coating*

Preheat oven to 300°F. In a medium mixing bowl, cream butter, sugar and vanilla. Blend several dots of orange icing color to creamed mixture. Add flour and mix until dough is smooth. Press in Mini Pumpkin Pan sprayed with vegetable pan spray. Bake pumpkins 15-20 minutes, or until very lightly browned. Cool 10 minutes in pans and remove shortbread to cool.

Melt Candy Melts according to package directions. Dip bottoms of cookies in melted candy. Fill disposable bag with Candy Melts, snip end of bag and pipe facial features.

Makes 4 dozen shortbreads.

*Halloween Cookie Cutters from Wilton let you create tricks and treats of every shape and size. From Giant Pumpkins to Bite-Size Bats, everyone will love decorating these things that go crunch in the night. And don't forget the Spooky Cookie Set, with 10 favorite frights in classic cookie size.*

# Jumpin' Pumpkin Cake

*Wilton Jack-O-Lantern Pan*

***Cake:***
*2 cups all purpose flour*
*2 teaspoons baking powder*
*1½ teaspoons pumpkin pie spice*
*1 teaspoon baking soda*
*¼ teaspoon salt*
*1 cup vegetable oil*
*1½ cups sugar*
*3 eggs*
*1 (16 oz.) can solid pack pumpkin*
*½ cups chopped nuts (optional)*

***Frosting:***
*Wilton Tip #18*
*Wilton Disposable Decorating Bag*
*4 cups (16 oz.) confectionery sugar, sifted*
*6 tablespoons butter*
*3-4 tablespoons half and half*
*1½ teaspoons maple flavoring*

Preheat oven to 350°F. Grease and flour Jack-O-Lantern Pan. Combine flour, baking powder, spice, soda and salt. In a separate bowl, beat oil, sugar and eggs. Stir in pumpkin, flour mixture, and nuts (if desired). Pour into prepared Jack-O-Lantern Pan. Bake on center rack 25-30 minutes or until an inserted cake tester comes out clean. Cool.

In a medium bowl, combine all frosting ingredients. Beat until smooth. Frosting recipe makes 2¼ cups, enough to cover pumpkin, if desired. To decorate as shown pipe tip #18, string eyes, nose and mouth. Pipe tip #18 zigzag stem.

Makes 15 servings.

# Spooky Raisin Bars

*Wilton 10½ x 15½ x 1 in. Jelly Roll/ Cookie Pan*

***Crust:***
*1 cup unsalted butter*
*2 cups all purpose flour*
*¼ cup sugar*

***Filling:***
*2½ cups firmly packed brown sugar*
*4 eggs*
*¼ cup all purpose flour*
*1 tablespoon Wilton Clear Vanilla*
*1 teaspoon baking powder*
*2 cups raisins*
*Wilton Candy Melts™*, Orange and Light Cocoa (1 cup each needed)*

**Brand confectionery coating*

Preheat oven to 350°F. In a medium mixing bowl, cream butter. Add flour and sugar and mix until dough is smooth. Spread in Jelly Roll/Cookie Pan. Bake 10 minutes or until lightly browned. For filling, combine sugar and eggs; mix. Add flour, vanilla and baking powder. Stir until blended. Stir in raisins. Pour over crust; bake 30 minutes or until filling is set. Cool. Melt Candy Melts colors separately, following package directions. Drizzle melted candy over top of crust. Let set 5 minutes; cut into bars.

Makes 30 servings.

*Make an easy candy Pumpkin Plaque using the Jack-O-Lantern Pan and Candy Melts.™ Simply melt the candy following package directions, paint eyes, nose and mouth in Cocoa and stem in Green, then pour melted Orange Melts to desired height to fill in the rest. Chill to set and unmold.*

# Pumpkin Patch Brownies

*Wilton Mini Pumpkin Pan*
*Wilton Orange Icing Color*
*Wilton Tip #2*
*Wilton Disposable Decorating Bags*
*½ cup butter or margarine, softened*
*1 cup sugar*
*2 eggs*
*1¼ cup unsifted all purpose flour*
*¼ cup unsweetened cocoa*
*¼ teaspoon baking soda*
*¾ cup chocolate syrup*
*1 teaspoon vanilla*
*½ cup chopped walnuts*
*Buttercream Icing (see pg. 19)*
*Chocolate cookie crumbs and candy worms*

**Brand confectionery coating*

Preheat oven to 350°F.

Cream butter or margarine, sugar and eggs in large mixer bowl until light and fluffy. Combine flour, cocoa and baking soda; add alternately with syrup to creamed mixture. Add vanilla. Stir in chopped walnuts. Spray Mini Pumpkin pan with vegetable oil spray. Pour batter into prepared pans. Bake for 30 minutes. Let cool and remove from pan. Using tinted orange buttercream, pipe tip 2 string facial features. Make a bed of "dirt," using fine chocolate cookie crumbs. Add candy worms.

Makes 8 mini brownies.

*For more Halloween chills, use the Mini Pumpkin Pan to make Sherbet Shockers! Outline the eyes, nose and mouth areas of pan cavities with chocolate syrup and place pan in freezer. When set, fill cavities with Orange sherbet and place back in freezer. Unmold perfect little pumpkins that go great with brownies!*

# Cranberry Salad

*Wilton Viennese Swirl Pan*
*1 lb. fresh cranberries*
*4 oranges — grind one with peel on, three without*
*1 (16 oz.) can crushed pineapple*
*2½ cups sugar*
*3 envelopes unflavored gelatin*
*Cranberries and orange slices for garnish*

In food processor with metal blade, process cranberries and oranges, do not over process — fruit should be coarse textured; add crushed pineapple. Strain and press juice out of fruit. Add sugar to fruit. Dissolve gelatin in one cup of cold juice. Heat remainder of the juice, add gelatin mixture, and stir until dissolved. When cool, add to fruit mixture. Rinse Viennese Swirl Pan with cold water and pour mixture into mold. Refrigerate overnight. To unmold, run small flexible spatula around edge of mold. Dip in hot water for 3-4 seconds. Invert on serving plate. Garnish with orange slices and fresh cranberries.

Makes 18-20 servings.

# Blueberry Snack Cake

*Wilton Viennese Swirl Pan*
*¾ cup butter, softened*
*1 cup sugar*
*3 eggs*
*1½ teaspoons Wilton Clear Vanilla*
*1½ cups flour*
*1½ teaspoons baking powder*
*⅓ teaspoon baking soda*
*⅓ teaspoon salt*
*¾ cup sour cream*
*1½ cup blueberries, fresh or frozen*
*¾ cup brown sugar*
*1½ teaspoons cinnamon*
*1½ cups chopped pecans*

An easy to make cake, perfect for Thanksgiving morning breakfast or brunch.

Preheat oven to 350°F. Grease Viennese Swirl Pan with solid vegetable shortening and dust with flour or use a vegetable pan spray.

Place butter and sugar in large mixing bowl, cream until light and fluffy, add eggs and vanilla, beat. Toss flour, baking powder, baking soda and salt with fork. Add alternately with sour cream to cream mixture. Mix until smooth. Toss brown sugar, cinnamon and nuts together.

Pour half the batter into prepared pan. Mix blueberries and half the brown sugar, cinnamon and nut mixture, spread over batter; add remaining batter. Top with other half of nut mixture. Bake 30-40 minutes or until toothpick comes out clean. Cool 10 minutes, remove from pan. This can be served swirled side up garnished with berries and softly whipped cream or with the nut/cinnamon crust side up. To bake the night before serving, bake, remove from pan and cover. Serve at room temperature or reheat briefly in a 350°F oven.

Makes 12 servings.

*This easy salad is an elegant alternative to sliced cranberry sauce. Made in our Viennese Swirl Pan, it's a graceful shape perfect for your Thanksgiving buffet. The versatile Viennese Swirl Pan is also ideal for whipped gelatin molds, rice pilaf or cakes.*

# Sweet Potato Pie

*Wilton 9 in. Pie Pan with Drip Rim*
*Wilton 10 x 15 in. Cookie Sheet*
*Wilton Maple Leaf Cookie Cutter*
*Pastry for 2 crust pie*
*3 tablespoons butter*
*¾ cup sugar*
*3 cups mashed sweet potatoes*
*4 eggs, separated*
*1 cup milk*
*1 teaspoon Wilton Clear Vanilla*
*½ teaspoon freshly grated nutmeg*
*½ teaspoon cinnamon*
*¼ teaspoon cloves*
*Dash salt*

Preheat oven to 350°F. Line 9 in. Pie Pan with half of pastry. Cream butter and sugar. Beat in sweet potatoes, egg yolks, milk, vanilla, seasonings and salt. In a separate bowl, beat egg whites until stiff; fold whites into potato mixture. Pour into pastry shell. Bake 50 minutes or until knife inserted near center comes out clean.

To decorate pie, cut remaining pastry into leaf shapes with cutters. Bake at 400°F for 9 to 11 minutes or until lightly browned. Place on top of pie before serving.

Makes 6 to 8 servings.

# Brandy Chocolate Pecan Pie

*Wilton 9 in. Pie Pan With Drip Rim*
*Pastry for 1 crust pie*
*3 eggs*
*½ cup firmly packed lightly brown sugar*
*1½ cups light corn syrup*
*4 tablespoons butter, melted*
*1 tablespoon brandy or 1 teaspoon vanilla*
*3 ounces semisweet chocolate, finely chopped*
*1 cup pecan halves*
*1 9 in. unbaked pie shell*

Preheat oven to 350°F. Line 9 in. Pie Pan with pastry. Beat eggs until foamy; add sugar, corn syrup, butter and brandy. Mix well. Stir in chocolate. Arrange pecan halves in bottom of pie shell. Carefully pour filling into pie shell. Bake 40 to 45 minutes or until filling is firm to the touch. Cool. If desired, decorate with whipped cream and chocolate curls.

Makes 6 to 8 servings.

*Forget the mess on Thanksgiving! With the Wilton 9 in. Pie Pan with Drip Rim, your fruit, pumpkin, pecan or sweet potato pies won't spill into your stove and burn. The wide edge makes it easy to remove, too.*

# Pumpkin Bread Pudding

*Wilton 6 in. Springform Pans (2 needed)*
*Wilton Disposable Decorating Bags*
*Wilton Tip #21*
*16 slices day-old bread*
*2 cans (12 oz. each) evaporated milk*
*1½ cups brown sugar*
*2 teaspoons pumpkin pie spice*
*1 can (16 oz.) solid pack pumpkin*
*6 eggs, lightly beaten*
*1 cup chopped walnuts*
*1 cup whipping cream, whipped*

Preheat oven to 325°F. Grease bottom and sides of two 6 in. Springform Pans. Cut bread into cubes and put into a large mixing bowl. Combine evaporated milk, brown sugar, pumpkin pie spice, pumpkin and eggs in saucepan. Heat over medium heat, stirring constantly until mixture is warm and slightly thickened (about 7 to 8 minutes). Pour warm mixture over bread cubes, stir well and let stand 3 minutes. Stir in walnuts. Divide bread mixture evenly between the two prepared pans. Place pans on a cookie sheet. Bake at 325° F for 1 hour and 15 minutes to 1 hour and 20 minutes, or until a knife inserted near the center comes out clean. Cool 30 minutes in pan, then remove and serve warm or chill to serve later. Garnish with whipped cream piped with tip #21 and additional chopped walnuts. Serve with remaining whipped cream.

Makes 12 servings.

*There's no time like Thanksgiving for special cheesecake desserts, made quick and easy in two Wilton 6 in. Springform Pans. Simply divide your favorite cheesecake recipe between the pans, and before serving, top one with cranberry sauce, the other with a dusting of cinnamon and chocolate curls. Delicious!*

# Cherry Star Tarts

*Wilton Mini Muffin Pan*
*Wilton Nesting Star Cookie Cutters*
*1 (28 oz.) can cherry pie filling*
***Basic Pastry Recipe:***
*2¼ cups flour*
*1 teaspoon salt*
*½ cup cold butter*
*¼ cup shortening*
*5-6 tablespoons cold water*

Make Basic Pastry Recipe (recipe may also be used for any double crust pie): Combine flour and salt in bowl or in work bowl of food processor fitted with metal blade. Cut butter and shortening into flour with pastry blender or on/off pulses of food processor until mixture resembles coarse meal. Add water a few tablespoons at a time until dough just holds together. Form into two flat disks and refrigerate at least 30 minutes. Roll on lightly floured surface into 12 x 12 in. square, ⅛ in. thick. Cut with 3½ in. star cutters; reroll to complete desired number of stars.

Preheat oven to 375°F. Place stars on *back* of Mini Muffin Pan. Pastry will form around pan as it bakes. Prick bottom with fork. Bake 7-10 minutes or until brown. Cool 1-2 minutes and remove. Cool and fill with pie filling. Garnish with chopped almonds and mint leaves. Shells can also be filled with lemon mousse (see pg. 71) or with a crabmeat salad (see pg. 16) for an appetizer. Shells can be stored 2-3 days in an airtight container.

Makes approximately 24 shells.

# Spritz Cookies

*Wilton Spritz Cookie Press Set*
*Wilton Red Crystal, Green Crystal, Rainbow Nonpareils Sprinkle Decorations*
*Wilton Cookie Sheet*
*1½ cups butter or margarine*
*1 cup granulated sugar*
*1 egg*
*2 tablespoons milk*
*1 teaspoon Wilton Clear Vanilla Extract*
*½ teaspoon Wilton Almond Extract*
*4 cups all-purpose flour*
*1 teaspoon baking powder*

Preheat oven to 400°F. Thoroughly cream butter and sugar. Add egg, milk, vanilla and almond extract; beat well. Stir together flour and baking powder; gradually add to creamed mixture, mixing to make a smooth dough. Do not chill. Place dough into cookie press and press cookies onto ungreased cookie sheet. Decorate with Wilton Sprinkles. Bake 6 to 8 minutes; remove cookies from sheet. Cool on rack.

Makes 6 dozen cookies.

*Open presents on Christmas morning over warm muffins made in Wilton's Mini Muffin Pan. It's the perfect "finger food" size—especially welcome when everyone's hands are busy tearing open the gifts!*

# Chicken Artichoke Mousse With Pistachio Pastry

***Mousse***
*Wilton Treeliteful Pan*
*1 lb. cooked chicken, cut into bite size pieces*
*2 jars (3 oz. each) marinated artichoke hearts, undrained, tough leaves trimmed*
*½ cup mayonnaise*
*2 tablespoons Dijon-style mustard*
*1 teaspoon salt*
*½ teaspoon pepper*
*2 packets unflavored gelatin*
*½ cup cool chicken broth*
*1 cup whipping cream, whipped*
*Herbs, cranberries, fresh artichoke for garnish*

Combine chicken, artichokes and liquid, mayonnaise, mustard, salt and pepper in food processor or blender. Process to puree mixture. Transfer to large mixing bowl. In a separate bowl, sprinkle gelatin over chicken broth, let set 2-3 minutes, heat until clear. Stir gelatin into pureed mixture. Fold in whipped cream until well blended. Spray Treeliteful Pan with vegetable oil nonstick coating spray. Spread chicken mixture evenly into pan. Refrigerate several hours or overnight until set. To unmold, run thin bladed knife around edge of pan, dip in hot water 2-3 seconds. Unmold onto serving platter and garnish with herbs, cranberries, and artichoke. Serve with pistachio pastry cutouts.

Makes 8-10 servings

***Pastry***
*Wilton Bite-Size Christmas Cookie Cutter Set*
*Wilton Cookie Sheet*
*2 cups all-purpose flour*
*2 teaspoons sugar*
*¼ teaspoon salt*
*⅔ cups finely ground natural pistachio nuts*
*⅔ cups butter or margarine*
*4-6 tablespoons cold water*

Preheat oven to 400°F. Combine flour, sugar, salt and nuts in medium mixing bowl. Cut in butter with pastry blender until mixture resembles small peas. Stir in cold water gradually with a fork just until pastry holds together. Shape together into two balls of dough. Roll out pastry, one ball at a time, between sheets of plastic wrap to ¼-⅜ in. thickness. Cut out shapes with Bite-Size Christmas Cutters. Bake on ungreased cookie sheet for about 10 minutes or until lightly browned. Cool.

Makes about 4 dozen pastries.

*For a more festive presentation, make your holiday fruitcake in The Treeliteful Pan. Gelatin, ice cream molds and all kinds of cakes will turn out beautifully in Treeliteful—and you can add miniature candies or glazed fruit for great-looking ornaments!*

# Banana Ginger Fruit Cake

*Wilton 10 in. Fancy Ring Mold Pan or Wilton Petite Fancy Ring Mold Pans (2 needed)*
*1 package (6 oz.) chopped, mixed, dried fruit (1½ cups)*
*4 cups sifted all-purpose flour, divided*
*1 cup (2 sticks) butter or margarine*
*1½ cups sugar*
*4 eggs*
*1½ cups mashed ripe bananas (about 4 medium)*
*1 teaspoon Wilton Clear Vanilla*
*2 teaspoons baking soda*
*1 teaspoon ground ginger*
*½ teaspoon salt*
*1 cup buttermilk*

***Holly Decorations***
*Wilton Leaf Green, Christmas Red Icing Colors*
*Wilton Tips 3, 352*
*Buttercream Icing (see pg. 19)*

***Sugar Glaze***
*1¼ cup confectioners sugar*
*3 tablespoons milk*

Preheat oven to 325°F. Grease and flour 10 in. Fancy Ring Mold or two (12 cavities total) Petite Fancy Ring Mold Pans. Combine dried fruit pieces and ½ cup flour; set aside. Combine butter and sugar in a large mixer bowl. Beat with electric mixer until creamy. Beat in eggs, one at a time, beating well after each addition. Stir in bananas and vanilla extract. Combine remaining 3½ cups flour, baking soda, ginger and salt. Stir into creamed mixture, alternating with buttermilk, ending with flour mixture. Stir in reserved fruit; mix just until blended. Pour mixture into prepared pan(s), dividing evenly if using Petite Pans. Bake for 1 hour to 1 hour 5 minutes for 10 in. Fancy Ring Mold or 35-40 minutes for Petite Fancy Ring Mold pans or until cake tester comes out clean. Cool cake 10 minutes in pan(s); invert and remove from pan(s). Cool completely; dust with confectioners sugar, or glaze and decorate.

To glaze, stir milk into sugar; drizzle mixture over cake. Tint buttercream icing, gradually adding a few drops of icing color until desired color is reached. Using tip 352, pipe holly leaves, add tip 3 dot berries.

Makes one 10 in. Ring Mold Cake or twelve Petite Ring Mold Cakes. Glaze recipe makes ½ cup.

*Homebaked gifts are easiest to make before the busy holiday season begins. This cake can be made ahead, wrapped without icing and frozen for up to 4 months! Use the Petite Fancy Ring Pans, and you'll make 12 gifts at once! When the holidays arrive, you'll have plenty of gifts on hand for teachers, friends, and family.*

Season's Greetings

# Blue Cheese Spread

*Wilton Viennese Swirl Pan*
*2 tablespoons unflavored gelatin*
*3/4 cup cold water*
*1/2 cups hot milk*
*2 (8 oz.) packages cream cheese*
*2 cups sour cream*
*12 oz. blue cheese*
*3 tablespoons white wine Worcestershire sauce*
*1/2 teaspoon white pepper*
*3 tablespoons finely grated onion*

Lightly oil Viennese Swirl Pan. Soften gelatin in cold water; stir in hot milk. Cool. In large bowl, beat cream cheese, sour cream, blue cheese, Worcestershire sauce, pepper and onion until well blended. Stir in gelatin mixture. Pour into prepared pan. Refrigerate several hours or overnight. To remove from pan, carefully loosen edges with a small spatula and invert onto serving plate. Garnish and serve with pear and apple slices, star fruit and assorted crackers. For a bridal shower, garnish with lemon leaves and pink rose petals.

Makes 30-40 appetizer servings.

# Orange Chocolate Torte

*Wilton Viennese Swirl Pan*
*1 1/2 cups (3 sticks) butter, cut in 1/2 in. pieces*
*6 oz. unsweetened chocolate, chopped*
*6 eggs, separated*
*2 1/2 cups granulated sugar*
*1 1/4 cups all-purpose flour*
*1 cup chopped pecans*
*3 tablespoons Grand Marnier or other orange-flavored liqueur*
*1 1/4 teaspoons Wilton Clear Vanilla*
*2 tablespoons grated orange zest*
*1/4 teaspoon salt*

Preheat oven to 350°F. Grease bottom and sides of Viennese Swirl Pan.

Melt butter in top of double boiler or microwave; add chocolate; stir until melted and smooth. Remove from heat, cool slightly.

In a large mixing bowl, mix egg yolks and sugar until just blended; stir in chocolate mixture until smooth. Add flour, pecans, liqueur, vanilla and orange zest; stir. Do not use mixer or overmix. In a large mixer bowl, beat egg whites with salt until stiff, not dry.

Mix one fourth of egg whites into chocolate mixture to lighten; fold into remaining egg whites. Pour into prepared pan and bake 30-40 minutes or until a skewer inserted off center comes out clean. Cool ten minutes and remove from pan. Cool. Serve with lightly whipped cream. Garnish with strips of orange peel.

*For a special way to ring in the new, dress the Orange Chocolate Torte above in a gleaming Chocolate Ganache Glaze, using Wilton Candy Melts and whipping cream. You'll find the recipe on the Viennese Swirl Pan label.*

12

# GRAND FINALE TRUFFLE DESSERT

*Wilton Mini-Ball Pan*
*2 (14 oz.) packages Wilton Candy Melts™* — Dark Cocoa*
*Wilton Disposable Decorating Bags*
*2 cups whipping cream, divided*
*1 package frozen raspberries in syrup, thawed*
*2 tablespoons raspberry liqueur (optional)*

**Brand confectionery coating*

Thoroughly dry Mini-Ball Pan. Melt 1 package Candy Melts™ according to package directions. Divide between 6 pan cavities. With a clean pastry brush, brush candy up onto sides of pan. Refrigerate 5 minutes, repeat, continuing until candy forms a thin shell. Refrigerate 15 minutes, unmold onto a clean cloth.

For filling, heat 1 cup whipping cream on top of range or in microwave to just before boiling. Coarsely chop and add remaining bag of Candy Melts.™ Stir until smooth, add liqueur, let set at room temperature until pudding-like consistency. Whip until light and fluffy. For ease of handling, place chocolate shell back in Mini Ball Pan, fill with truffle mixture, smooth top. Refrigerate until firm or serving time. Unmold. If you plan to make more than six, unmold after firm and store in refrigerator rounded side up. Repeat for additional desserts.

To garnish as shown, make raspberry sauce by processing berries in blender or food processor. Strain to remove seeds if desired. Make a pool of raspberry sauce on plate. Whip remaining 1 cup cream until soft peaks form. Place softly whipped cream in uncut disposable bag (or a bag fitted with a #3 or #4 tip). Snip end of bag, make a circle of cream around outside of dessert. Pull points out with small knife or toothpick. You might want to try this on a small plate before preparing serving plates. Top desserts with chocolate curls and fresh raspberries.

Makes 6 desserts.

*The versatile Mini Ball Pan is an entertainer's best friend. The truffle dessert mold made above can be turned to serve as a bowl and filled with fresh fruit or ice cream and garnished with whipped cream. For children's parties the mold can be filled with crispy rice treats, inverted and decorated as festive party faces.*

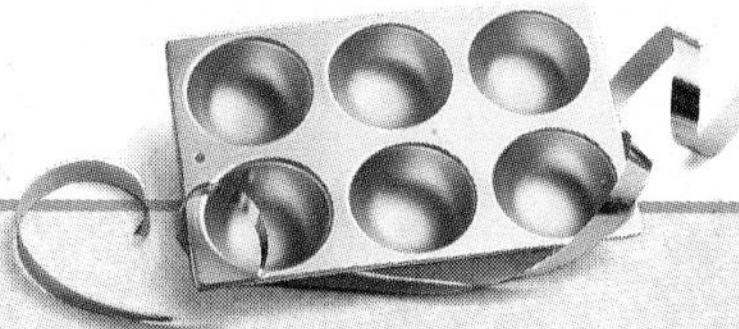

*Creative Director*..........Richard Tracy<br>
*Food Editor*...............Zella Junkin<br>
*Food Stylists*<br>
*and Decorators*.........Lois Hlavak<br>
Kim Hartman<br>
Lee Mooney<br>
Susan Matusiak<br>
Steve Rocco<br>
Mary Gavenda<br>
Corky Kagay<br>
*Photography*..............Kathy Sanders<br>
*Photo Assistant*...........Kathy Watt<br>
*Writers*...................Jeff Shankman<br>
Mary Enochs<br>
Marita Seiler<br>
*Production Coordinators*..Marie DeBenedictis<br>
Mary Stahulak


To order the Wilton Products used in this book, use the Order Form inside.
Those items not listed on the Order Form, such as tips and colors,
are available where Wilton products are sold. You can also write or call:


Wilton Enterprises<br>
Caller Service 1604<br>
2240 W. 75th St., Woodridge, IL 60517<br>
1-708-963-7100




For photography purposes, some designs were decorated with royal icing.


Printed in U.S.A.

*Wilton products used in this book are available through your Wilton dealer or the current Wilton Yearbook of Cake Decorating. You may also use this handy Order Form to purchase most products in this book.*

## How To Order

1 Print your name, address and phone number clearly. If you wish your order sent to another address, be sure to include that information in the area designated: "SHIP TO."

2 You may pay by check, money order or credit card (Only VISA, MasterCard or Discover Card accepted.) SORRY, NO C.O.D. ORDERS. To charge an order to your VISA, MasterCard or Discover Card enter your charge card number in the boxes. Supply card expiration date and your signature. Orders will not be processed without this information.

Make checks payable to Wilton Enterprises.

Wilton Enterprises is not responsible for cash sent by mail.

Orders from outside U.S.A. must be paid in U.S. Funds only.

3 Fill in the number of items desired. If an item includes more than one piece, DO NOT list number of pieces. Example: 14 piece set is listed as 1 item under quantity.

4 Total your order.

5 Add appropriate amount to your order for shipping, handling and postage for inside U.S.A. (See chart inside Order Form to determine charges.) Wilton ships via United Parcel Service. Allow 10 working days for delivery. (HI and AK allow 17 working days.)

Outside the U.S.A. shipping, handling and postage totals $7.00. Allow 3 months for delivery (except Canada).

(see other side)

## Order Form

(1) SOLD TO: (Please print plainly) BN

Name ______________________

Address ______________________

City ______________ State ______ Zip ______

Daytime Phone No./Area Code ______-______-______

SHIP TO: (Fill in only if different from Sold To.)

Name ______________________

Address ______________________

City ______________ State ______ Zip ______

Daytime Phone No./Area Code ______-______-______

(2) CREDIT CARD ORDERS: Use Visa, MasterCard, or Discover Card! Fill in the boxes: Credit Card Number

| | | | | | | | | | | | | | | | | | |
|---|---|---|---|---|---|---|---|---|---|---|---|---|---|---|---|---|---|

Expiration Month/Year ______ Signature ______________

PANS (3)

| STOCK NO. | HOW MANY | DESCRIPTION | PRICE OF ONE | TOTAL PRICE |
|---|---|---|---|---|
| 2105-A-9311 | | Angel Food Pan (7″) | $ 9.99 ea. | |
| 2105-A-2525 | | Angel Food Pan (10″) | $13.99 ea. | |
| 415-A-903 | | Cake Cover 9 x 13″ | $ 4.49 ea. | |
| 2105-A-1265 | | Cookie Sheet 10 x 15″ | $ 6.49 ea. | |
| 2105-A-6711 | | Cute Clown Pan | $ 9.99 ea. | |
| 2105-A-4793 | | Egg Pan Set, 3-D | $ 9.99 set | |
| 2105-A-9340 | | Embossed Heart Pan | $ 7.99 ea. | |
| 2105-A-2644 | | Even-Bake® Insulated Cookie Sheet 13 x 17″ | $14.99 ea. | |
| 2105-A-2646 | | Even-Bake® Insulated Cookie Sheet 10 x 15″ | $12.99 ea. | |
| 2105-A-5008 | | Fancy Ring Mold Pan (10″) | $ 9.99 ea. | |
| 2105-A-6504 | | First And Ten Football Pan | $ 9.99 ea. | |
| 2105-A-2023 | | Handsome Guy Pan | $ 9.99 ea. | |
| 2105-A-5176 | | Heart Pan (9″) | $ 5.99 ea. | |
| 2105-A-5168 | | Heart Pan (12″) | $ 8.99 ea. | |
| 2105-A-3254 | | Horseshoe Pan | $ 9.99 ea. | |
| 2105-A-4943 | | Huggable Bear Pan | $ 9.99 ea. | |
| 2105-A-3068 | | Jack-O-Lantern Pan | $ 7.99 ea. | |
| 2105-A-1269 | | Jelly Roll/Cookie Pan (10½ x 15½″) | $ 9.99 ea. | |
| 2105-A-1820 | | Jumbo Muffin Pan | $12.99 ea. | |
| 2105-A-2010 | | Little Lamb Pan Set | $10.99 set | |
| 2105-A-1588 | | Long Loaf Pan | $ 9.99 ea. | |
| 2105-A-9312 | | Mini Angel Food Pan | $14.99 ea. | |
| 2105-A-1760 | | Mini Ball Pan | $ 9.99 ea. | |
| 2105-A-4497 | | Mini Bear Pan | $ 9.99 ea. | |
| 2105-A-4426 | | Mini Bunny Pan | $ 7.99 ea. | |
| 2105-A-9331 | | Mini Dinosaur Pan | $ 9.99 ea. | |
| 2105-A-9791 | | Mini Loaf Pan | $ 9.99 ea. | |
| 2105-A-2125 | | Mini Muffin Pan | $ 7.99 ea. | |
| 2105-A-1499 | | Mini Pumpkin Pan | $ 7.99 ea. | |
| 2105-A-4396 | | Mini Shell Pan | $ 9.99 ea. | |
| 2105-A-9336 | | Numbers Pan Set | $19.99 set | |
| 2105-A-1280 | | Partysaurus Pan | $ 9.99 ea. | |
| 2105-A-1308 | | Performance Pans 9 x 13″ Sheet Pan | $ 7.99 ea. | |
| 2105-A-8213 | | Performance Pans 12″ Square | $10.99 ea. | |
| 2105-A-4794 | | Petite Egg Pan | $ 7.99 ea. | |
| 2105-A-2097 | | Petite Fancy Ring Mold Pan | $16.99 ea. | |
| 2105-A-2432 | | Petite Heart Pan | $ 7.99 ea. | |
| 2105-A-8462 | | Petite Jack-O-Lantern Pan | $ 7.99 ea. | |
| 2105-A-6811 | | Pie Pan w/Drip Rim (9″) | $ 6.99 ea. | |
| 2105-A-190 | | Ring Mold Pan (8″) | $ 6.99 ea. | |
| 2105-A-4013 | | Ring Mold Pan (10½″) | $ 7.99 ea. | |
| 2105-A-5602 | | Round Pan (8″) | $ 5.49 ea. | |

## Order Form

(1) SOLD TO: (Please print plainly) BN

Name ______________________

Address ______________________

City ______________ State ______ Zip ______

Daytime Phone No./Area Code ______-______-______

SHIP TO: (Fill in only if different from Sold To.)

Name ______________________

Address ______________________

City ______________ State ______ Zip ______

Daytime Phone No./Area Code ______-______-______

(2) CREDIT CARD ORDERS: Use Visa, MasterCard, or Discover Card! Fill in the boxes: Credit Card Number

| | | | | | | | | | | | | | | | | | |
|---|---|---|---|---|---|---|---|---|---|---|---|---|---|---|---|---|---|

Expiration Month/Year ______ Signature ______________

PANS (3)

| STOCK NO. | HOW MANY | DESCRIPTION | PRICE OF ONE | TOTAL PRICE |
|---|---|---|---|---|
| 2105-A-9311 | | Angel Food Pan (7″) | $ 9.99 ea. | |
| 2105-A-2525 | | Angel Food Pan (10″) | $13.99 ea. | |
| 415-A-903 | | Cake Cover 9 x 13″ | $ 4.49 ea. | |
| 2105-A-1265 | | Cookie Sheet 10 x 15″ | $ 6.49 ea. | |
| 2105-A-6711 | | Cute Clown Pan | $ 9.99 ea. | |
| 2105-A-4793 | | Egg Pan Set, 3-D | $ 9.99 set | |
| 2105-A-9340 | | Embossed Heart Pan | $ 7.99 ea. | |
| 2105-A-2644 | | Even-Bake® Insulated Cookie Sheet 13 x 17″ | $14.99 ea. | |
| 2105-A-2646 | | Even-Bake® Insulated Cookie Sheet 10 x 15″ | $12.99 ea. | |
| 2105-A-5008 | | Fancy Ring Mold Pan (10″) | $ 9.99 ea. | |
| 2105-A-6504 | | First And Ten Football Pan | $ 9.99 ea. | |
| 2105-A-2023 | | Handsome Guy Pan | $ 9.99 ea. | |
| 2105-A-5176 | | Heart Pan (9″) | $ 5.99 ea. | |
| 2105-A-5168 | | Heart Pan (12″) | $ 8.99 ea. | |
| 2105-A-3254 | | Horseshoe Pan | $ 9.99 ea. | |
| 2105-A-4943 | | Huggable Bear Pan | $ 9.99 ea. | |
| 2105-A-3068 | | Jack-O-Lantern Pan | $ 7.99 ea. | |
| 2105-A-1269 | | Jelly Roll/Cookie Pan (10½ x 15½″) | $ 9.99 ea. | |
| 2105-A-1820 | | Jumbo Muffin Pan | $12.99 ea. | |
| 2105-A-2010 | | Little Lamb Pan Set | $10.99 set | |
| 2105-A-1588 | | Long Loaf Pan | $ 9.99 ea. | |
| 2105-A-9312 | | Mini Angel Food Pan | $14.99 ea. | |
| 2105-A-1760 | | Mini Ball Pan | $ 9.99 ea. | |
| 2105-A-4497 | | Mini Bear Pan | $ 9.99 ea. | |
| 2105-A-4426 | | Mini Bunny Pan | $ 7.99 ea. | |
| 2105-A-9331 | | Mini Dinosaur Pan | $ 9.99 ea. | |
| 2105-A-9791 | | Mini Loaf Pan | $ 9.99 ea. | |
| 2105-A-2125 | | Mini Muffin Pan | $ 7.99 ea. | |
| 2105-A-1499 | | Mini Pumpkin Pan | $ 7.99 ea. | |
| 2105-A-4396 | | Mini Shell Pan | $ 9.99 ea. | |
| 2105-A-9336 | | Numbers Pan Set | $19.99 set | |
| 2105-A-1280 | | Partysaurus Pan | $ 9.99 ea. | |
| 2105-A-1308 | | Performance Pans 9 x 13″ Sheet Pan | $ 7.99 ea. | |
| 2105-A-8213 | | Performance Pans 12″ Square | $10.99 ea. | |
| 2105-A-4794 | | Petite Egg Pan | $ 7.99 ea. | |
| 2105-A-2097 | | Petite Fancy Ring Mold Pan | $16.99 ea. | |
| 2105-A-2432 | | Petite Heart Pan | $ 7.99 ea. | |
| 2105-A-8462 | | Petite Jack-O-Lantern Pan | $ 7.99 ea. | |
| 2105-A-6811 | | Pie Pan w/Drip Rim (9″) | $ 6.99 ea. | |
| 2105-A-190 | | Ring Mold Pan (8″) | $ 6.99 ea. | |
| 2105-A-4013 | | Ring Mold Pan (10½″) | $ 7.99 ea. | |
| 2105-A-5602 | | Round Pan (8″) | $ 5.49 ea. | |

# HOW TO ORDER CONTINUED

6 Add state and local taxes *where you live** to your total amount, including shipping and delivery charges. See Tax Chart below. Wilton Enterprises is required by law to collect state taxes on orders shipped to:

AZ 5%; CA 7.75%; CO 3.8%; FL 6%; GA 6%; IA 5%; IL 6.75%; IN 5%; KS 4.9%; KY 6%; LA 4%; MD 5%; MA 5%; MI 4%; MN 6.5%; MO 5.725%; NC 6%; NJ 6%; NY 7%; OH 6%; PA 6%; SC 5%; SD 6%; TN 8.25%; TX 8%; UT 6.25%; VA 4.5%; WA 7.5%.

*Tax rates are subject to change according to individual state legislation without notice.

7 UPS Next Day and Second Day Service available upon request. Air Service outside U.S.A. add 100% of your cost.

8 When your order arrives... Should you be missing an item from your order (1) check to be sure you have not overlooked the merchandise (2) check over your receipted order form. If any item is temporarily out of stock we forward the balance of your order with out of stock notification and the reorder date. If payment is check or money order, you will receive a credit memo for the amount of the missing item. The memo may be applied to your next order or returned to Customer Service for a cash refund. Charge Accounts will be charged only for merchandise shipped.

Wilton Return Policy: Inspect all merchandise upon arrival. If you're dissatisfied in any way with any item, notify Wilton Customer Service in writing with a copy of your invoice and all available information regarding your order before returning merchandise. A Customer Service Representative will contact you.

You have 60 days to return merchandise. Handle returns promptly, as they take approximately 30 days to process.

SAVE MAILING TIME! Phone in your charge order. 1-708-963-7100. Ask for mail order. Remember! Only charge orders (VISA, MasterCard or Discover Card) will be accepted by phone.

Prices in this book supersede all previous Wilton publications. Wilton reserves the right to change prices without notice.

For inquiries on your previous order, send all available information and a copy of your invoice to:

**Wilton Enterprises**
2240 West 75th Street
Woodridge, IL 60517
1-708-963-7100
*A Wilton Industries Company*

PANS ③

| STOCK NO. | HOW MANY | DESCRIPTION | PRICE OF ONE | TOTAL PRICE |
|---|---|---|---|---|
| 2105-A-5619 | | Round Pan (9") | $ 5.99 ea. | |
| 2105-A-8250 | | Shell Pan | $ 9.99 ea. | |
| 2105-A-6506 | | Sports Ball Pan Set | $ 9.99 set | |
| 2105-A-4437 | | Springform Pan (6") | $ 7.99 ea. | |
| 2105-A-5354 | | Springform Pan (9") | $10.99 ea. | |
| 2105-A-5611 | | Square Pan (8") | $ 7.99 ea. | |
| 2105-A-425 | | Treeliteful Pan | $ 7.99 ea. | |
| 2105-A-8252 | | Viennese Swirl Pan | $ 9.99 ea. | |
| CANDY | | | | |
| 1911-A-358 | | Candy Melts—Dark Cocoa (14 oz. bag) | $ 2.50 ea. | |
| 1911-A-544 | | Candy Melts—Light Cocoa (14 oz. bag) | $ 2.50 ea | |
| 1911-A-1631 | | Candy Melts—Orange (14 oz. bag) | $ 2.50 ea. | |
| 1911-A-447 | | Candy Melts—Pink (14 oz. bag) | $ 2.50 ea. | |
| 1911-A-499 | | Candy Melts—Red (14 oz. bag) | $ 2.50 ea. | |
| 1911-A-498 | | Candy Melts—White (14 oz. bag) | $ 2.50 ea. | |
| 1913-A-1299 | | Candy Colors Kit | $ 3.99 kit | |
| 710-A-812 | | Sprinkles—Green Crystal (4½ oz. pk.) | $ 1.99 pk | |
| 710-A-802 | | Sprinkles—Rainbow Jimmies (4½ oz. pk.) | $ 1.99 pk. | |
| 710-A-800 | | Sprinkles—Rainbow Nonpareils (4½ oz. pk.) | $ 1.99 pk. | |
| 710-A-813 | | Sprinkles—Red Crystal (4½ oz. pk.) | $ 1.99 pk. | |
| COOKIES | | | | |
| 2304-A-1521 | | Alphabet Cutter Set (26 pc.) | $ 8.99 set | |
| 2303-A-9317 | | Bite-Size Christmas Cutter Set (5 pc.) | $ 2.49 set | |
| 2303-A-9314 | | Bite-Size Western Cutter Set (5 pc.) | $ 2.49 set | |
| 2304-A-90 | | Jack-O-Lantern Cutter Set (4 pc.) | $ 2.99 set | |
| 2304-A-1532 | | Bear Nesting Cookie Cutters (4 pc.) | $ 2.99 set | |
| 2304-A-115 | | Heart Nesting Cookie Cutters (6 pc.) | $ 2.99 set | |
| 2304-A-113 | | Round Nesting Cookie Cutters (6 pc.) | $ 2.99 set | |
| 2304-A-111 | | Star Nesting Cookie Cutters (6 pc.) | $ 2.99 set | |
| 2303-A-109 | | Clown Perimeter Cookie Cutter | $ .69 ea. | |
| 2303-A-107 | | Maple Leaf Perimeter Cookie Cutter | $ .69 ea. | |
| 2104-A-4000 | | Spritz Cookie Press | $10.99 set | |
| OTHER | | | | |
| 604-A-2126 | | Almond Extract (2 oz.) | $ 1.79 ea. | |
| 1003-A-3121 | | Bomboniere!® ⁵⁄₁₆" Instant Bow Ribbon Pink (4 yds.) | $ 3.99 pk. | |
| 604-A-2237 | | Clear Vanilla Extract (2 oz.) | $ 1.79 ea. | |
| 201-A-1450 | | Crystal-Look Base | $ 2.99 ea. | |
| 2104-A-9355 | | Decorator Brush Set (3) | $ 1.49 set | |
| 2104-A-358 | | Disposable Decorating Bags (12 pk.) | $ 3.99 pk. | |
| 2104-A-1358 | | Disposable Decorating Bags (24 pk.) | $ 6.29 pk. | |
| 399-A-1009 | | Wooden Dowel Rods (pk. of 12) | $ 2.49 pk. | |
| 399-A-801 | | Plastic Dowel Rods (pk. of 4) | $ 2.29 pk. | |
| 202-A-402 | | Love's Duet Ornament (Black Tux) | $11.99 ea. | |
| 702-A-6007 | | Meringue Powder (4 oz.) | $ 4.49 ea. | |
| 702-A-6015 | | Meringue Powder (8 oz.) | $ 6.99 ea. | |
| 415-A-680 | | Parchment Paper Roll (15" x 33 ft.) | $ 4.99 ea. | |
| TOPPERS | | | | |
| 710-A-475 | | Baseball Mitt Icing Decorations (9 pc.) | $ 1.99 pk. | |
| 710-A-476 | | Basketball Icing Decorations (9 pc.) | $ 1.99 pk. | |
| 2811-A-9124 | | Gold Jumbo Candles (8 pc.) | $ 1.49 pk. | |
| 2113-A-1818 | | Happy Graduate Topper | $ 2.09 ea. | |

**MONEY BACK GUARANTEE** If you are not completely satisfied with your Wilton purchase, return the item for an exchange or refund.

4 TOTAL MERCHANDISE
5 ADD SHIPPING, HANDLING & POSTAGE CHARGE. NOTE! Find the amount you pay on chart below.
6 STATE AND LOCAL TAXES—SEE TAX NOTE
SPECIAL SHIPPING SERVICES
7 SUBTOTAL
8 COUPONS AND/OR CREDIT MEMO DEDUCTIONS
TOTAL AMOUNT ENCLOSED

FOR OFFICE USE ONLY. Please do not write in space below.

| Date | Cash | Debit M. | Credit M. | Hndlng Charge |
|---|---|---|---|---|
| Air Mail | Foreign | Pal/Sam | Coupon | Gift Ct. |

Shipping and Handling Charges (See No. 5)
Orders up to $29.99 ...... add $3.75
Orders from $30-49.99... add $4.50
Orders from $50-74.99... add $5.50
Orders $75 and more...... add $6.50

PANS ③

| STOCK NO. | HOW MANY | DESCRIPTION | PRICE OF ONE | TOTAL PRICE |
|---|---|---|---|---|
| 2105-A-5619 | | Round Pan (9") | $ 5.99 ea. | |
| 2105-A-8250 | | Shell Pan | $ 9.99 ea. | |
| 2105-A-6506 | | Sports Ball Pan Set | $ 9.99 set | |
| 2105-A-4437 | | Springform Pan (6") | $ 7.99 ea. | |
| 2105-A-5354 | | Springform Pan (9") | $10.99 ea. | |
| 2105-A-5611 | | Square Pan (8") | $ 7.99 ea. | |
| 2105-A-425 | | Treeliteful Pan | $ 7.99 ea. | |
| 2105-A-8252 | | Viennese Swirl Pan | $ 9.99 ea. | |
| CANDY | | | | |
| 1911-A-358 | | Candy Melts—Dark Cocoa (14 oz. bag) | $ 2.50 ea. | |
| 1911-A-544 | | Candy Melts—Light Cocoa (14 oz. bag) | $ 2.50 ea | |
| 1911-A-1631 | | Candy Melts—Orange (14 oz. bag) | $ 2.50 ea. | |
| 1911-A-447 | | Candy Melts—Pink (14 oz. bag) | $ 2.50 ea. | |
| 1911-A-499 | | Candy Melts—Red (14 oz. bag) | $ 2.50 ea. | |
| 1911-A-498 | | Candy Melts—White (14 oz. bag) | $ 2.50 ea. | |
| 1913-A-1299 | | Candy Colors Kit | $ 3.99 kit | |
| 710-A-812 | | Sprinkles—Green Crystal (4½ oz. pk.) | $ 1.99 pk | |
| 710-A-802 | | Sprinkles—Rainbow Jimmies (4½ oz. pk.) | $ 1.99 pk. | |
| 710-A-800 | | Sprinkles—Rainbow Nonpareils (4½ oz. pk.) | $ 1.99 pk. | |
| 710-A-813 | | Sprinkles—Red Crystal (4½ oz. pk.) | $ 1.99 pk. | |
| COOKIES | | | | |
| 2304-A-1521 | | Alphabet Cutter Set (26 pc.) | $ 8.99 set | |
| 2303-A-9317 | | Bite-Size Christmas Cutter Set (5 pc.) | $ 2.49 set | |
| 2303-A-9314 | | Bite-Size Western Cutter Set (5 pc.) | $ 2.49 set | |
| 2304-A-90 | | Jack-O-Lantern Cutter Set (4 pc.) | $ 2.99 set | |
| 2304-A-1532 | | Bear Nesting Cookie Cutters (4 pc.) | $ 2.99 set | |
| 2304-A-115 | | Heart Nesting Cookie Cutters (6 pc.) | $ 2.99 set | |
| 2304-A-113 | | Round Nesting Cookie Cutters (6 pc.) | $ 2.99 set | |
| 2304-A-111 | | Star Nesting Cookie Cutters (6 pc.) | $ 2.99 set | |
| 2303-A-109 | | Clown Perimeter Cookie Cutter | $ .69 ea. | |
| 2303-A-107 | | Maple Leaf Perimeter Cookie Cutter | $ .69 ea. | |
| 2104-A-4000 | | Spritz Cookie Press | $10.99 set | |
| OTHER | | | | |
| 604-A-2126 | | Almond Extract (2 oz.) | $ 1.79 ea. | |
| 1003-A-3121 | | Bomboniere!® ⁵⁄₁₆" Instant Bow Ribbon Pink (4 yds.) | $ 3.99 pk. | |
| 604-A-2237 | | Clear Vanilla Extract (2 oz.) | $ 1.79 ea. | |
| 201-A-1450 | | Crystal-Look Base | $ 2.99 ea. | |
| 2104-A-9355 | | Decorator Brush Set (3) | $ 1.49 set | |
| 2104-A-358 | | Disposable Decorating Bags (12 pk.) | $ 3.99 pk. | |
| 2104-A-1358 | | Disposable Decorating Bags (24 pk.) | $ 6.29 pk. | |
| 399-A-1009 | | Wooden Dowel Rods (pk. of 12) | $ 2.49 pk. | |
| 399-A-801 | | Plastic Dowel Rods (pk. of 4) | $ 2.29 pk. | |
| 202-A-402 | | Love's Duet Ornament (Black Tux) | $11.99 ea. | |
| 702-A-6007 | | Meringue Powder (4 oz.) | $ 4.49 ea. | |
| 702-A-6015 | | Meringue Powder (8 oz.) | $ 6.99 ea. | |
| 415-A-680 | | Parchment Paper Roll (15" x 33 ft.) | $ 4.99 ea. | |
| TOPPERS | | | | |
| 710-A-475 | | Baseball Mitt Icing Decorations (9 pc.) | $ 1.99 pk. | |
| 710-A-476 | | Basketball Icing Decorations (9 pc.) | $ 1.99 pk. | |
| 2811-A-9124 | | Gold Jumbo Candles (8 pc.) | $ 1.49 pk. | |
| 2113-A-1818 | | Happy Graduate Topper | $ 2.09 ea. | |

**MONEY BACK GUARANTEE** If you are not completely satisfied with your Wilton purchase, return the item for an exchange or refund.

4 TOTAL MERCHANDISE
5 ADD SHIPPING, HANDLING & POSTAGE CHARGE. NOTE! Find the amount you pay on chart below.
6 STATE AND LOCAL TAXES—SEE TAX NOTE
SPECIAL SHIPPING SERVICES
7 SUBTOTAL
8 COUPONS AND/OR CREDIT MEMO DEDUCTIONS
TOTAL AMOUNT ENCLOSED

FOR OFFICE USE ONLY. Please do not write in space below.

| Date | Cash | Debit M. | Credit M. | Hndlng Charge |
|---|---|---|---|---|
| Air Mail | Foreign | Pal/Sam | Coupon | Gift Ct. |

Shipping and Handling Charges (See No. 5)
Orders up to $29.99 ...... add $3.75
Orders from $30-49.99... add $4.50
Orders from $50-74.99... add $5.50
Orders $75 and more...... add $6.50